A true gift for anyone looking to write a horror screenplay. Jamie Nash knows the genre inside and out and has broken down the tropes into forms and functions that are fully understandable, easy to implement, and utterly effective. All you need to add is your own creative inspiration, which this terrific book will spark.

– Craig Perry, Producer, the *Final Destination* and *American Pie* franchises, *Breaking In*

Scary good! This book takes the dread out of writing horror and replaces it with tools that are not only practical but wildly inspiring. It's like having a co-writer who knows exactly how to unlock the fear in your story and the fun in your process. A must-have for horror fans and creators alike.

– Eduardo Sánchez, Director/Co-Writer, *The Blair Witch Project*; Director, *Exists*, *Lovely Molly*, *Hysteria!*, *Goosebumps*, *From Dusk Till Dawn: The Series*

You'll learn something about your craft from *Save the Cat! Writes Horror*. It's compulsively readable and full of smart, actionable advice whether you're a seasoned pro or just starting out your horror career.

– Adam Cesare, Author, *Clown in a Cornfield, Influencer*

Jamie Nash has written yet another indispensable resource for the aspiring screenwriter. *Save the Cat! Writes Horror* is an extraordinary high-level overview of all the pieces necessary to make something great, memorable, and, above all, terrifying.

– Kyle Brett, Creative Executive (Film), Blumhouse Productions

This book is the writing partner that saves you from scrapping six months of work over one unnoticed misstep on page five. No rigid rules here—just the perfect gentle question asked at exactly the right time. It's wild that they're giving this away for the price of a book. Any serious horror writer should be willing to sell their soul for dark magic like this.

– Daniel Stamm, Director, *The Last Exorcism*, *Prey for the Devil*, *Them*

The monster at the end of this book is the horror story you write after reading it.

– Stephen Graham Jones, Author, *The Only Good Indians, My Heart Is a Chainsaw*

Save the Cat! Writes Horror completely demystifies the horror screenwriting process by breaking down the genre to its elemental state and allowing the individual to build it back up in the image of their own subjective fears and desires.

– Sean Keller, Writer, *The Last Voyage of the Demeter, Giallo, Rage*

– Chelsea Stardust, Director, *Satanic Panic, All That We Destroy*; Producer, *Into the Dark*

Save the Cat! Writes Horror is not only Nash's love letter to his wheelhouse genre, but an astute examination of the cinematic things that go bump in the night. A first-rate book for film buffs, genre junkies, and anyone who grew up gnawing their knuckles in front of a late-night horror movie. This is a book that demands to be added to your collection.

– Ronald Malfi, Author, *Come With Me, Small Town Horror*

Jamie Nash is a certified horror nerd who brilliantly and effortlessly delivers a master class on horror. He expertly entertains and enlightens us while unpacking the core elements inside a terrific horror script, providing everything you need when you sit down to write.

– Sheila Hanahan Taylor, Co-Founder, Practical Pictures. Past projects include the *American Pie* and *Final Destination* franchises, *Breaking In*, *Repli-Kate*, and *Oddball.* Sheila also mentors at the Film Independent Episodic Lab, ran the Fox TV Writers Lab, and has been an instructor at UCLA Film School for over 25 years.

SAVE THE CAT!® WRITES HORROR

The Ultimate Guide to Creating Monster in the House Stories

JAMIE NASH

Based on the Books by

Blake Snyder

Published in the United States by *Save the Cat!*® Press,
Los Angeles, CA

www.savethecat.com

Cover Design: Scott Higgins
Interior Design: Gina Mansfield Design
Editor: Brett Jay Markel

Library of Congress Control Number: 2025938643
Trade Paperback ISBN: 978-0-9841576-5-5
ebook ISBN: 978-0-9841576-8-6

Printed in the United States of America

TABLE OF CONTENTS

THE OPENING SCARE

When I was a kid, I loved to scare people.

My house was the only one on the block that didn't have a fence. My backyard was the neighborhood shortcut. It was dark back there. Woods, shadows... and who knows what.

When the sun went down and the streetlights flickered weakly against the void, my friends would have to go home for the night.

Which meant they'd have to take the shortcut.

Cue the spooky music.

I'd get my favorite werewolf mask... the one that smelled like rubber and Three Musketeers...

And wait...

And wait...

And wait...

Then I'd scare the bejesus out of them.

Yeah, I had problems.

This was the early 1980s. Every weekend, UHF Television (look it up if you were born after 1988) served me a regular diet of R-rated horror movies. Watching a little black-and-white TV with a big rabbit-eared antenna, my eyeballs devoured movies not meant for nine-year-olds: *Halloween*, *Night of the Living Dead*, *The Exorcist*, *The Omen*, all the *Godzilla* movies, *It's Alive!*, and a healthy dose of *Dark Shadows* episodes. I saw most of the *Nightmare on Elm Street* franchise in the mall multiplex (back then they were very loose about letting 12-year-olds into R-rated movies and most of our parents didn't care or didn't notice).

I was there for the opening night of *Fright Night*, *The Lost Boys*, and *The Thing*. My favorite TV episodes had a horror flavor... like that creepy Hawaii Tiki doll two-parter *The Brady Bunch* did with Vincent Price or that *Gilligan's Island* episode where ghosts haunted the castaways. I chomped on Count Chocula while watching *Scooby-Doo* and loved those Abbott and Costello movies with Frankenstein and Dracula, and even talked my dad into taking me to see *Young Frankenstein* when it showed up at our local drive-in a few years after its initial release.

I was also a scared kid. One of my earliest memories was being utterly petrified by that Anthony Hopkins *Magic* trailer. It didn't help that I owned a creepy ventriloquist dummy that watched over me every night when I fell asleep. *Shudder*. I was also terrified of rollercoasters and roller skating and thunderstorms and those weird creaks coming from the attic at midnight. Existential dread plagued me too. I worried about sabotaged trick-or-treat candy, lurking serial killers, nuclear war, and alien invasion.

Weirdly though, I begged to go to my church's annual Halloween Haunted House and tapped out after the first strobe light flipped on and some Grim Reaper-looking thing with a chainsaw came charging at me.

And yet, I kept chasing the horror. Drawn to it. Like one of Dracula's wives under the thrall of his undead magnetism.

Part of it was a way to manage the fear. To push my limits. To slowly expose myself bit by bit to things that made me uncomfortable.

Books became an easy way to modulate the fear. In grade school, I'd read novelizations of *Halloween 2* and *The Fog* and leafed through a graphic novel of *Alien* (made by the *Heavy Metal* people) so many times it split in half. Around fifth grade, I dove deep into Stephen King, Peter Straub, Dean R. Koontz, and eventually Clive Barker.

Then I started to make horror.

Looking back, I think it was the ultimate way to tame all those fears. Instead of being scared, I'd be the *scarer*! What started with scaring people in the backyard evolved into plotting out haunted houses in my friends' basements.

Mine were always more like interactive theater with stories and escalation and bad acting. I made a dozen of 'em before I turned 16. I also played the recurring Jason Voorhees in a more professional one. Then came homemade VHS movies, edited VCR to VCR, and a bunch of short stories I wrote, an aborted novel or two, a few *Call of Cthulhu* campaigns, 16mm films... and then came screenplays.

The screenplay that broke my writing career was a horror one. I've since written over 100 scripts in every genre imaginable, but more than half of them are horror. I've authored horror novels. I've worked on theme park haunted houses. I've directed horror movies and podcasts. And I still write at least one scary movie or novel a year.

And that's why this book exists.

For the last couple of decades, I've been both a student and a teacher of the craft of screenwriting (and storytelling) and if you've ever met me in person or taken one of my classes, you know most of my examples come from Stephen King or Wes Craven or R.L. Stine. I co-host a podcast about screenwriting and the vast majority of our movies are Monster in the House flicks.

This was a book I was destined to write. I'm not sure if writing horror is a way I still control the scary parts of life or if I'm still that kid hiding behind the tree... waiting and waiting in the shadows...

Either way, let's hide behind the tree together...

Put on that mask...

And wait... and wait... and wait...

INTRODUCTION: WHY HORROR?

Every year, some low-budget movie comes out of nowhere and out performs a half-a-billion-dollar budgeted blockbuster and someone says, "Horror is baaaaack!"

Dude. It's not back. It never goes away. Never. At least not recently. Or maybe not since the 70s.

When Blake Snyder was selling specs in the early 90s, horror was in a bit of a slump. The studios had burnt through all those 80s horror franchises. *Friday the 13th*, *Halloween*, *Nightmare on Elm Street* had all run their course. It wouldn't be long before all of us horror geeks were pitching *Halloween vs. Hellraiser* (true story, btw) in a desperate attempt to resuscitate the old favorites.

Then Hollywood began experimenting. Studio horror crept on the scene—stuff that felt a little cleaner and safer and PG-13er than the video nasties I watched as a kid. Even *Freddy vs. Jason* got a big budget.

And guess what? Horror was baaaaaaack!

Next came the reboot phase, found footage, the return of zombie movies, the torture porn, the J-Horror, the elevated horror wave, the Stephen Kingaissance, the zombies again, the zombies, more zombies...

Even in recent years, as movie theaters have been dominated by big budget sequels and adaptations of already popular books, videogames, and comics, there's one genre where original ideas and lower-budget productions are still profitable and often post at the top of the box office.

And yeah, that's horror.

For spec screenwriters looking to break into the biz, horror's where it's at. And while other genres retreat to streamers and VOD, horror movies still play on the big screen because they're visceral and experiential and fun to see in a dark room with a big crowd of screaming fans. Original stories, low budgets, no IP necessary... producers need these projects. They need writers. So if you're going to be a screenwriter, you can't make a better bet than horror.

Horror films have been a great "first gig" for many top filmmakers. In recent times, you can look back to James Gunn, James Wan, Leigh Whannell,

Anna Lily Amirpour, David F. Sandberg, Karyn Kusama, and Adam Wingard. Back in the day, John Carpenter, Sam Raimi, Kathryn Bigelow, Guillermo Del Toro, Kevin Williamson, Stephen Spielberg, and many more got their start in horror before moving on to other genres.

Because horror can be a good way to "break in," some aspiring scribes who aren't even down with horror dabble in it. And while I don't encourage any writer to force themselves to crank out stories they dislike or don't understand or even loathe, I'd encourage my non-horror-leaning peers to be open to giving horror a chance.

The genre is so vast in tone and topic that it seems only the most nightmare-sensitive writer or the highest of high-brow artists could not find something that jives with their tastes. There are films as varied as *Hereditary* and *The Menu* and *M3GAN* and *Talk to Me* and *Skinamarink* and *Terrifier* and *I Saw the TV Glow*. There are "scare-every-10-minute" James Wan-produced blockbusters and the A24 slow burn dread fests that are as interested in real pathos as they are in monsters and ghouls.

If you're a dabbler in the dark genre, I urge you to sample a wide gallery of horror shows, films, and books to find an intersection with your own storytelling. If you don't like the visceral thrills of *Halloween* or *Don't Breathe*, maybe you'll prefer the atmospheric weirdness of *Midsommar*, or the art-house psychological tension of *The Light House*, or the sheer audacity of *Barbarian* or *The Substitute*. I'm positive there's a horror movie that you'd like and I'm sure there's one you'd love to write.

Okay, enough of the jibber-jabber.

The monster is waiting for us.

Lurking in the pages that follow.

Let's dim the lights and step into the shadows.

PART 1: THE BUILDING BLOCKS OF HORROR

CHAPTER 1: WHAT IS HORROR?

In recent years, a lot of online cineastes have fought the "What is horror?" war. Think pieces abound. Genre aficionados debate which movies are horror and which are not. Some are non-horror critics claiming that anything "quality" somehow isn't horror. Others are of the mindset, "It didn't scare me, so it's not horror." I've heard other litmus tests like: "If it's primarily meant to scare, it's horror." Or "If it's not supernatural, it's not horror."

So where do I come down?

What's my hot take?

Here goes: *If you think it's horror, it's horror.*

At their most primal, horror stories are about survival—whether it's survival of identity, free will, or physical life—set against a backdrop of isolation and pursued by a relentless menace that won't stop until the hero is dead. *The Exorcist*, *Halloween*, *The Walking Dead*, *A Quiet Place*, *It*... these are my horror movies.

Stories with horror tropes or tones which have engines that aren't specifically focused on survival, isolation, and monsters make me squint a little. *The Mummy* (be it Brendan Frasier or Tom Cruise), the *Underworld* series, *The Munsters*, or *Hotel Transylvania*—these might be other genres mixing in dark tones and horror atmospheres and characters. Nothing wrong with that. I love it. One of my favorite things about Sam Raimi and Peter Jackson is how they bring so much horror goodness to their blockbuster action and fantasy films. But *Dr. Strange in the Multiverse of Madness* and *Lord of the Rings* are not horror movies.

In the original *Save the Cat!* book, Blake Snyder outlined his 10 storytelling genres. Unlike typical "video store" genres (Drama, Sci-Fi, Comedy, Action, Romance, Horror, etc.), Blake's genres were less about tone and audience expectations and more about common "plots" and patterns to execute those plots. They're a tool that guides the writer and focuses their plotting on a tried-and-true throughline.

Here's a quick look at those genres:

BUDDY LOVE – These are those "you complete me" stories. A spiritually incomplete hero finds a companion who somehow makes them more whole. Because of a complication, the two struggle to be together in the way they're meant to be. Buddy Love movies are your love stories, friendship stories, mother/daughter stories, and boy-and-their-dog stories. Examples: *Challengers, The Peanut Butter Falcon, The Farewell, Zootopia, Brokeback Mountain, When Harry Met Sally, Bad Boys*

DUDE WITH A PROBLEM – An innocent hero is yanked into a life-or-death problem and, despite massive odds against them, must overcome it. Many stories are about dudes with problems. But the keys to this genre are innocent underdogs who are undeservingly pulled into a predicament and forced to react. Examples: *Don't Look Up, Die Hard, The Martian, Hunger Games, Taken, North by Northwest*

FOOL TRIUMPHANT – An underestimated "fool" is pitted against an establishment but proves their hidden value to everyone, causing them to triumph! Fool Triumphant stories are about heroes who don't fit in but can teach us something about life. Examples: *Elf, Poor Things, King Richard, Boogie Nights, The King's Speech, Legally Blonde, Being There*

GOLDEN FLEECE – A hero and their team embark on a quest to win a prize or accomplish a mission. Sports movies, quests, and road trips are the stuff of the Golden Fleece genre. There should be a clear "prize" or "finish line" that the audience can track. But a Golden Fleece is always about something internal—a hero goes "on the road" in search of one thing and winds up discovering something else: themselves. Examples: *Top Gun: Maverick, The Mitchells vs. the Machines, Raiders of the Lost Ark, Dodgeball, Little Miss Sunshine, 1917, Harold & Kumar Go to White Castle*

INSTITUTIONALIZED – A hero is entrenched inside a certain group, institution, or establishment. These stories are about how the hero struggles to fit into the system. They must decide if being part of the group is worth the effort and ultimately must choose to join, leave, or destroy the institution. Workplace stories and stories about institutions or establishments are the hallmarks of institutionalized storytelling. Examples: *The Holdovers, Air, The Devil Wears Prada, Full Metal Jacket, Office Space, One Flew Over the Cuckoo's Nest*

RITES OF PASSAGE – A hero suffering through a relatable life problem (divorce, growing up, death, mid-life crisis, etc.) tries to solve it by avoidance instead of tackling it head-on. Like most heroes, they choose the wrong path and ultimately need to learn the hard way. Examples: *Anora, The Fabelmans, CODA, Ordinary People, Bridesmaids, Lost in Translation, Birdman*

OUT OF THE BOTTLE – An ordinary hero's life is changed by magic that either bestows a wish or a power or inflicts them with a curse. Whichever way, this magic changes the hero's life and makes things difficult. The magic is resolved in the end, but the lesson it teaches resonates with the hero forever. Examples: *Soul, Groundhog Day, Freaky Friday, Click, Bruce Almighty, Big, Liar Liar, Field of Dreams*

SUPERHERO – A hero with a superpower (or important mission) faces a potent nemesis or catastrophic problem so large it challenges even their mighty powers. These movies are about extraordinary people tested by the values of the world. Examples: *Deadpool, Black Panther, The Woman King, Superman, Spider-Man, Erin Brockovich,* James Bond movies

WHYDUNIT – A hero/detective pursues a case where the real puzzle is "why" the case proves so compelling that (s)he is willing to dive into the darkness to find the answer. Examples: *Se7en, Blade Runner, Body Heat, The Big Lebowski, Chinatown*

And then there's one more:

MONSTER IN THE HOUSE – A hero is trapped in some location or situation (a.k.a the house) and must survive a monster (human or otherwise). Monster in the House stories are commonly found in horror movies, urban thrillers, or comedies about people or things that just won't go away. Examples: *Psycho, Jaws, The Conjuring, The Exorcist, A Quiet Place, It, Get Out*

As you might guess, both from the description above and the title of this book, the Monster in the House—or MITH for short—is the stuff of horror movies. Monsters and isolation. Stories of survival.

There are three fundamental elements of Monster in the House stories:

1.) A **monster** that is supernatural in its powers—even if its strength derives from insanity or determination.

2.) A **house** that traps the hero. It can include a family unit, an entire town, or even "the world."

3.) A **sin** that lets the monster in... a transgression that can include ignorance.

As you might guess, in Blake Snyder's original books, every horror movie he breaks down falls into the MITH category.

So, while not all Monster in the House stories are horror stories (comedies about annoying people who just won't go away like *What About Bob?* and *Cable Guy* come to mind, or even dramas where people are trapped with people who are psychological monsters like *Whiplash*), *Halloween*, *Friday the 13th*, *Saw*, *Nightmare on Elm Street*, *Child's Play*, *Alien*, *Jaws*, *Texas Chainsaw Massacre*, *It*, *Scream*, *The Thing*, *A Quiet Place*, *Candyman*, *Night of the Living Dead*, *Evil Dead*, etc., etc.—all fall into the MITH box with its 3 elements: **monster**, **sin**, and **house**.

So, every horror movie is a Monster in the House, right? Well, that's what I used to think. Until one dark and stormy night...

I co-host a podcast called *Writers/Blockbusters* where we break down movies to find screenwriting lessons. We analyzed Jordan Peele's *Nope*. *Nope* is a horror movie. It's scary. It's got a monster. There's a battle for survival and lots of terrifying set pieces and creepy weirdness.

Monster in the House, right?

Well...

Whenever I analyze movies, the first question I ask is "What's the pitch? What's the spine or Story DNA? a.k.a. Who is the *hero*? What's their *goal*? What's the enormous *obstacle* in their way? If they fail, what happens (a.k.a the *stakes*)?

In *Nope*, the Story DNA is:
Hero: A down-on-his-luck horse trainer
Goal: To get photographic evidence—The Oprah Shot—of a UFO that's menacing his ranch
Obstacle: The UFO and the difficulty of capturing a UFO on film
Stakes: Financial, mostly. He's in danger of losing the ranch that's been the pride of the family for years.

So, whaddya think? Is this a Monster in the House?

It has a **monster**, for sure.

It has a **house**: the UFO seems confined to an area around the ranch.

It even has a **sin**: exploiting creatures and even terrible events for spectacle is a theme that runs throughout the movie.

But here's the addendum I think Monster in the House requires: the victims should be *trapped* in the house. It's this absence of the hero being able to just walk away, which really is the hallmark of horror and is key to the Monster in the House genre. If you can "just leave," it's no longer a survival story. If you can tap out at any time without much grief, it's not that scary. Something needs to take that option off the menu.

I think *Nope* leans toward the Golden Fleece genre with its 3 elements of road, team, and prize. The characters are chasing a prize: getting the picture of the monster. There's a team. The journey is the process to get it, the quest. The plot is closer to a heist movie.

A lot of horror has procedural elements—plots play out like cop stories or Whydunits. *Jaws* feels this way at times. The third *Conjuring* movie is essentially a detective story. Same with *Longlegs*. But in these movies, unlike *Nope*, someone's trapped and helpless, even if it's not the hero. So while the hero isn't trapped, per se, they're the assigned protector of the victims and if they personally don't keep trying to stop it, the killing will continue.

Clive Barker's original *Hellraiser* had a huge influence on me. The pitch for *Hellraiser* could be summarized with the following Story DNA:

Hero: An unfaithful wife
Goal: To return her lover to flesh and blood by offering sacrifices
Obstacle: She's not a killer by nature but needs to lure the sacrifices in without her husband or daughter-in-law knowing what she's doing
Stakes: Being without her lover

The movie does some weird twists switching protagonists in the middle and becoming a more conventional Monster in the House in the second half. But the story's premise is really about a forlorn woman trying to resurrect her lover.

Again, this heroine isn't trapped. She could run away and never come back to the attic or somehow just let her lover stay dead. The house is in no way a prison, and the plot is not a survival story. If anything, she's teaming up with the monster, becoming the monster herself. She's the one that "brings the horror"—so much so there's a Hero Switch by the end of the story. Nevertheless, early on, she's our POV character and from that perspective, the story is probably more of a Golden Fleece or a Dude with a Problem genre.

Marvel's *Werewolf by Night* TV movie focuses on a group of monster hunters who are invited to hunt a creature in a winner-takes-all competition for a precious prize. Competitions to win trophies are the stuff of Golden Fleece stories. But again, the story has a monster (a couple in this case), a sin, and a house.

Some stories have horror tropes and monsters but aren't trying to scare at all. Things like the *Underworld* films or *Constantine* or *What We Do in the Shadows* have monsters, but the goals of these films aren't survival and the heroes tend to have more freedom than those in a real-deal Monster in the House film.

So, am I really saying *Nope* and *Hellraiser* aren't horror movies?

No. Not at all.

I'm pointing out that there's an important lesson for horror writers here. The *Save the Cat!* genres help identify the type of story you're telling and highlight essential aspects of structure and character. While the plots of films like *Nope* and *Hellraiser* align more closely with genres like Golden Fleece or Dude with a Problem, the stories still incorporate all the key elements of the Monster in the House (MITH) genre.

So, if you're writing a horror story that falls into Golden Fleece or Buddy Love or any of the other *Save the Cat!* genres, make sure your story includes the three key MITH components: a monster, a house, and a sin. Movies like *Nope*, *Hellraiser*, and *Werewolf by Night* all meet the MITH requirements. Stories that don'texplicitly follow a "battle for survival" plot might instead be hybrids, combining elements of genres like Golden Fleece or others with Monster in the House elements.

I'll add one additional box to the horror movie checklist: **all horror movies ultimately devolve into battles of survival.**

Even though these other genres or combo-hybrids begin as contests or quests or missions and their heroes can quit or give up the quest without someone dying... by the time the Finale rolls around, the heroes of these stories are indeed trapped with a monster and must 100% focus on staying alive. In the end, all of these stories devolve into Man vs. Monster. There's no option to tap out, to pack things up and go home. The hero is in a life-or-death battle... even if it comes a little late.

So, to summarize, make sure your story has:

1. A monster
2. A house
3. A sin that brings about the monster
4. A battle for survival – At some point, be it early in the story or late, the horror must devolve into a real battle of survival.

In the next few chapters, we'll take a deeper dive into each of the elements of the MITH genre.

EXERCISES

1. Make a list of your 5 favorite horror films or novels. What are their monster, house, and sin elements? Do these stories ultimately become a battle for survival?

2. If you have an idea for your own horror story, list or brainstorm its monster, house, and sin?

CHAPTER 2: THE MONSTER

All horror movies have monsters.

All of them.

Whether it's a serial killer with a chainsaw, a vengeful sleep demon with a razor glove, or some miracle anti-aging formula with soul-sucking side effects, **the monster** will always be at the heart of your Monster in the House.

Monsters can also take on the form of curses and inflictions... or sometimes, those types of inflictions cause the hero to become the monster.

Just to get a feel for the range and variety that monsters have in horror movies, here's a list of **monster types:**

1. GHOSTS – Ghosts are spirits of the dead who have not moved on from the world of the living. Examples: *Talk to Me, The Ring, The Woman in Black, The Grudge*
2. KILLER ANIMALS – Nature gone primal. Make the shark territorial or give the bear the taste for blood and you have a monster. Examples: *Cocaine Bear, Jaws, Cujo, Anaconda*
3. DEMONS – Sinister entities that exist to cause harm or spread their evil ways. Examples: *The Exorcist, Insidious, The Conjuring 2, Host*
4. ZOMBIES – Reanimated corpses that hunger for human flesh. Examples: *Night of the Living Dead, Dawn of the Dead, World War Z, Zombieland, The Walking Dead*
5. VAMPIRES – Vampires are undead creatures that drink blood to survive. Examples: *Nosferatu, Dracula, Twilight, Abigail, Last Voyage of the Demeter, Sinners*
6. WERE-MONSTERS – Humans who can transform into monstrous creatures (usually wolves). Examples: *An American Werewolf in London, The Howling, Hemlock Grove, Ginger Snaps*
7. HUMANOIDS – Humans or animals that are genetically messy, resulting in abnormal physical features or abilities. Examples: *The Hills Have Eyes, The Descent, Barbarian*

8. SCIENCE GONE WRONG – Monsters created by scientific accidents or the misuse of science. Examples: *Splice, Frankenstein, M3GAN, Re-Animator*

9. ALIENS – Creatures from other planets that are often portrayed as hostile to humans. Examples: *Alien, The Thing, A Quiet Place, Signs, Invasion of the Body Snatchers*

10. PSYCHO KILLERS – Human beings who orchestrate or commit multiple murders over time, driven by a specific motive, philosophy, set of rules, or reasons that remain unknown. Examples: *Psycho, Halloween, Scream, X, Longlegs, Heretic, Saw*

11. CULTS – Groups who follow a charismatic leader or ideology and engage in extreme or dangerous practices. Examples: *Rosemary's Baby, The Wicker Man, Midsommar, Green Room, Get Out*, *Last Night at Terrace Lanes*

12. POSSESSED OBJECTS – Inanimate objects that are possessed by evil spirits or demons. Examples: *Christine, Annabelle, The Amityville Horror, Ouija, Wishboard*

13. MUNDANE MENACES – When everyday things become monsters. Those things normally aren't terrifying but have intelligence and cunning that go beyond what we think. Examples: the killer plants in *The Happening, The Ruins*, and *Attack of the Killer Tomatoes,* and the murderous car tire from *Rubber*

14. WITCHES AND WARLOCKS – People who practice magic or make deals with demons or the devil. Examples: *The Blair Witch Project, The Witch, Suspiria*

15.UNEARTHED ABOMINATIONS – Monsters and behemoths born of this Earth but defying classification. Often of the Cryptozoological persuasion. Sometimes mutated beasts, but usually something that's been uncovered or awakened after long being dormant. Examples: *The Creature from the Black Lagoon,* Bigfoot in *Exists,* and various iterations of *Godzilla*

16.MYTHOLOGICAL MONSTERS – Monsters that come from mythology, cultures, or lore. Some are supernatural creatures that aren't even depicted as monsters per se but are when they get the horror makeover. Examples: *Silent Night, Deadly Night*; *Leprechaun*; *Krampus*; *Pan's Labyrinth*; *Trollhunter*; *Elves*

17. CLOWNS – Clowns are often depicted as playful and humorous, but in horror movies, they can be twisted and terrifying. Sometimes human. Sometimes alien. Sometimes something pure evil. Examples: Art the Clown from *Terrifier*, Pennywise from *It*, *Killer Klowns from Outer Space*, the clownpires from *The Night Watchmen,* and Frendo from *Clown in a Cornfield*

18. PSYCHOLOGICAL DEMONS – Psychological horror movies often explore the human mind and its limits. These demons afflict a major character, sometimes the hero. Examples: *Black Swan*, *Shutter Island*, and *Jacob's Ladder,* which have psychological demons affecting the heroes

19. COSMIC MONSTERS – Cosmic horror deals with the fear of the unknown and the idea that the universe is vast and uncaring. Examples: *The Call of Cthulhu*, *Event Horizon*, *Color Out of Space*

20. BIO-MONSTERS – Physical decay or transformation of the human body, be it disease or mutation or something that takes over and disrupts the body. Examples: *The Fly*, *Cabin Fever*, *28 Days Later*, *The Substance*

21. SUPERNATURAL CURSES – These malevolent forces are inflicted upon individuals through supernatural means, often as punishment for a perceived wrongdoing or violation of an unwritten rule. They can stem from a ritual, a spoken hex, or simply crossing paths with the wrong entity. The cursed individual is usually trapped in an escalating cycle of torment that can only be broken through extraordinary sacrifice, redemption, or outsmarting the curse itself. Examples: *Final Destination*, *Drag Me to Hell*, *Thinner*, *It Follows*

The above list gives you a broad range of monster types that can menace your stories, yet some monsters don't quite fit into the exact types. Sometimes monsters are a mix of these types, and there are surely other types or more specific categorizations. There are some tips at the end of this chapter for brainstorming a new type of monster. But for now, there's still more to "flesh out" to make your monster unique.

MONSTER LORE/BACKSTORY

Some horror stories keep the origins and the motives of their monsters mysterious. No one understands why Michael Myers is on a slasher spree in the original *Halloween*. *The Blair Witch Project* keeps both the monster and the true nature of it in the shadows. Stories like *The Thing* and *Cloverfield* play out in the HP Lovecraft tradition of "we can't understand what they are or why they're doing it." Movies like *The Ring* or *It* are all about digging up the monster's history to find a way to beat it. Other movies like *Annabelle* or *Child's Play* open with origin stories of the evil right at the start.

Defining your monster's backstory is important even if you never reveal it. Backstory questions always come up in pitch meetings and during development. Creative executives love to ask, "Well, where does it come from?" or "What's its plan?"

Sometimes producers or studio folks just need to know there's a method to all the madness, and everything isn't purely random and lazy writing. I've had many a meeting where I explained the monster's backstory but insisted that it never be revealed in the movie. Sometimes it's enough to make it clear that your ambiguity is a choice.

Coming up with your **monster's backstory** will help you craft your story. Even with a Lovecraft-style monster that can't be explained, it's best that you, the writer, have a working theory on it—if for no other reason than to help you plot your monster's diabolical ways.

To help flesh out your monster's lore, consider the following back-story questions:

1. ORIGIN – Where does the monster come from? What's the origin and where does the monster normally live? What does it normally do? Maybe it's from an alien planet? Maybe it has been frozen in a block of ice for centuries?

2. MOTIVE – Why is it on its current rampage? Is it out for some kind of revenge, like Jason Voorhees? Does it need to feast, like zombies and vampires? Is it just mindless and evil? Often the answers here will be tied to the origin.

3. TRIGGER – Why now? What triggered this monster to go on its current reign of terror? Usually, this is tied to the Monster in the House's sin. We'll go deeper into the sin in Chapter 4.

4. BANISHING METHOD – How can someone ultimately beat the monster? Does the monster have an Achilles heel? Is there some ritual to banish the monster? Can you give it what it wants so it'll go away? Or somehow trick it?

5. METAPHOR – Monsters are stand-ins for real-life horrors. They represent things we might actually be fearful of: death, the dark, parent-

hood, grief, technology, sex, etc. Is it loneliness as in *Let the Right One In*? The dangers of atomic weapons as in *Godzilla*? Or grief as in *The Babadook*? How does the monster fit into the overall theme or message of the movie? What real-world fear or problem does the monster stand in for?

The difference between **lore** and backstory is lore isn't always reliable. Lore is like a book with pages torn out. Most horror stories deliver their monster knowledge by word of mouth, ancient impartial texts, and speeches by amateur experts who have done some research but never faced the beast. While it's helpful for you to know the answers to your monster's backstory, you may choose to reveal something very different to your characters or audience. The information you dish out might be incomplete... or maybe you'll keep your audience completely in the dark about your monster's sinister history and ways.

MAKING YOUR MONSTER

The next step is to figure out your monster's appearance and how they carry out their monstrous deeds. Here are some key traits to help you craft your monster:

1. PHYSICAL ATTRIBUTES – What is the monster's physical appearance? Is it humanoid or animalistic? What are its size and shape? What color is its skin or fur? How does the evil thing get around? Does it slither, crawl, fly, or walk on two or more legs? Does it move silently or make a lot of noise? If it's a human... is there something that distinguishes it? Think of cosplayers and Halloween costumes—what are the props, masks, and clothes that cosplayers will gather to play your monster at the next HorrorCon?

2 ATTACK METHOD – How does the monster kill its victims? Does it use brute force or a more subtle approach? Does it have any special abilities or weapons? Is it an animal that gnaws at your hero? Does it spit acid? Does it wear knife-fingered gloves or carry a chainsaw? Or maybe it toys with its prey, setting up puzzles to torture and torment? Similar to the appearance, how can you freshen old tropes—a new weapon, a new strategy, a new innate ability to kill?

3 DREAD ALERT – How can the audience tell when the monster is nearby? Does it emit a distinctive sound, leave a scent, or cause other physical signs? If it's a curse, maybe a wind blows, or a light flickers. If it's a disease, maybe there's bleeding or blisters or over-dilated pupils. My buddy, script consultant Jimmy George a.k.a. the Script Butcher, pointed me

to these. He calls 'em "shark fins" because... well, *Jaws*. These dread alerts create tension in the audience and sometimes in the characters, too.

4. WEAKNESS – What is the monster's weakness? Is there something that can harm or kill it, such as sunlight, silver, or a particular type of weapon? Is there a way to temporarily escape it? Think of the monsters who can only hear but not see in *A Quiet Place* and *Don't Breathe*, or the limitations of the monster in *Lights Out*, where the creature can only kill in darkness. Or even vampires or the monsters of *The Descent* that are harmed by bright light. These might not be the ways the monster is finally slayed or banished—they're more limits on the beast, often determining where, when, or how it can attack.

MONSTER-TUDE

It might seem odd to think your monster has a personality, but when you think of Freddy Krueger, Jason Voorhees, Chucky, or Pinhead, you can see that monsters have a wide range of characteristics. Some monsters are heroes in their own minds who think what they're doing is noble and just. Others are bent on revenge, and still others are primal and seem programmed to kill.

Here are the common **monster personality types**:

1. THE RELENTLESS HUNTER – This is an unstoppable pursuer of their victims, such as the iconic slasher villains like Michael Myers from *Halloween* or Jason Voorhees from *Friday the 13th*. It also could be a curse as in *Drag Me to Hell* or *The Ring* or death itself in *Final Destination*.

2. THE VENGEFUL EVIL – This personality type represents restless spirits seeking revenge or retribution for past wrongdoings or killers out for revenge like Freddy Krueger in *The Nightmare on Elm Street* films. Movies like *The Grudge* or *Insidious* often feature vengeful spirits as the principal antagonists. The Blind Man from *Don't Breathe* seeks his own demented form of justice.

3. THE SADISTIC TORTURER – These monsters derive pleasure from inflicting pain and torment on their victims. They like to play with their food and make a game of their violence. Think of Jigsaw from the *Saw* franchise, Pennywise from *It*, or *The Collector*.

4. THE RAGING BEAST – This personality type is associated with monstrous creatures that unleash their animalistic instincts, such as werewolves or killer animals like *Cujo* or the Xenomorphs from *Alien*.

5. THE DEMENTED PSYCHOPATH – These monsters are driven by madness or psychopathic tendencies, relishing the violence. Examples include Norman Bates from *Psycho*, Leatherface from *The Texas Chainsaw Massacre*, Annie Wilkes from *Misery*.

6. MONSTERS ON A MISSION – Monsters with duties or codes that require carnage and mayhem in pursuit of their goals. Examples include the Cenobites like Pinhead from *Hellraiser* or in *Leprechaun*, where the monster is driven to protect his pot of gold.

When I'm defining my monster, I like to jump back and forth between these categories. Sometimes the creature's origin can inform the personality, or at other times, the personality can suggest the attributes. Bounce around the monster categories, letting one inform the other until you think you have a handle on your entire monster.

BUILD-A-BEAST: CREATING YOUR NEW MONSTER

If you're in the market for inventing a new monster or coming up with a fresh idea, mixing and matching the monster elements in this chapter can deliver some cool results. Here are some suggestions:

1. OLD MONSTER, NEW SETTING – Choose one of the monster types and put them in a new setting or house. Fresh ideas have come from placing a Cosmic Monster in space or a serial killer in a boarding school. Maybe you could place some vampires in the Deep South or on the Santa Carla boardwalk or an American werewolf in London!
2. MONSTER MASHUP – Maybe a vampire serial killer or a ghost witch or a demon-possessed cat or an alien possession story or, as we did on *The Night Watchmen*... Clownpires!
3. OLD MONSTER, NEW ORIGIN STORY OR LORE – Sometimes it's enough to give the monsters completely different origin stories. What if werewolves were caused by a bioweapon? What if werewolves were aliens? What if a cult was formed after an encounter with vampires?

Okay. So, you have a monster with a look and a lore and an insidious personality. It's time—after the exercises below—to put your monster in a house!

EXERCISES

1. Invent a New Monster Type
   a. Use the list of monster types provided in this chapter. Select attributes from different monster types and combine them to create a hybrid creature. For example, you might combine the relentless pursuit of a psycho killer with the supernatural abilities of a demon. Write a brief character profile for this hybrid monster, including its origin, appearance, and attack methods.
   b. Take an existing monster type and place it in an unexpected setting. For example, how would a ghost operate in a futuristic space station? What challenges would a werewolf face in a bustling city? Write a short scene or outline that explores how the setting impacts the monster's behavior and the story's dynamics.
2. Build-a-Beast – Either brainstorming the new monster you created in exercise #1 above or for a monster you're already working on for your own story, answer the following questions:
   a. What's the monster type from the list above?
   b. Where does your monster come from? What's its origin?
   c. What motivates it to do its "evil"?
   d. What triggers its current rampage?
   e. How can it be banished or defeated? What's its weakness?
   f. What real-world fear or problem does it symbolize?
3. Design your monster's appearance and traits – Focus on the physical and behavioral characteristics of your monster:
   a. Sketch or describe its appearance in detail.
   b. How does it move?
   c. What's its attack method?
   d. What sounds or signs indicate its presence?
   e. What unique features make it memorable and terrifying?
4. Pick a personality – Choose a monster personality type for your monster from the provided list (e.g., The Relentless Hunter, The Vengeful Evil, The Sadistic Torturer).
   a. Develop a scene that showcases this monster personality in action and outline it in a few sentences.
   b. How does this personality type influence the monster's interactions with its victims?
5. Lore and Misconceptions – Create a piece of lore or legend about your monster that the characters in your story believe to be true.

CHAPTER 3: THE HOUSE

Horror stories force heroes to face their ultimate fears. Protagonists can't escape. They can't get help. They alone must deal with the evil.

The primary reason for **the house** in the Monster in the House genre is to answer the following two questions about your story:

1. Why is there no obvious/easy way for your heroes to escape the horror?
2. Why is there no obvious/easy way for your heroes to get help?

You need to trap your heroes with your monster. But the house isn't necessarily a physical one. For every haunted house, abandoned building, and derelict spaceship, there are other less geographic places where monsters run rampant—like the mind/soul (*American Psycho, Eraserhead*) or the body (*The Fly*, *The Substance*, *Jennifer's Body*). Sometimes the monster just has enormous reach and there's simply nowhere to hide and no one who can help (*Final Destination*, *Drag Me to Hell*, *It Follows*).

If you're still brainstorming your House, here is a list of some common **house types** that each present distinct traps for the hero:

1. THE REMOTE LOCALE – Places where the nearest safety isn't reasonably close, perhaps hours or days away. Even if you could call for help, it would never arrive in time and the thought of getting to safety by foot is a sick joke. Examples include the Overlook Hotel in *The Shining*, the underground caves of *The Descent*, or any cabin-in-the-woods stories like *Evil Dead* or *Cabin Fever*.

2. THE PLACE NO ONE DARES TO GO – The cursed woods, the haunted mansion, or Dracula's castle—these are places full of red flags and warnings like the abandoned nuclear tainted grounds in *Chernobyl Diaries*, the asylum in *Session 9*, or the abandoned mental hospital in *Grave Encounters*. In these stories, even if you could call for help, no one would dare come to the rescue. Just entering these places means you're on your own.

3. ISLAND OF TERROR – Being stranded on a boat or in an underwater facility, like in *Open Water,* or in outer space like *Event Horizon*, or on the haunted boat of *Last Voyage of the Demeter* or even in the high perches of a stuck ski-lift in *Frozen* or the vertigo-inducing tower in *Fall.*

4. ALTERNATE REALITY – Being trapped in a time loop like *Happy Death Day* or in some virtual reality like *The Thirteenth Floor* or in a parallel universe like *Silent Hill*—even the idea of someone entering or leaving the alt world seems impossible.

5. THE PRISON – Being trapped in an actual prison or confined setting—like the sealed-off offices of *The Belko Experiment*, the deadly puzzle rooms of *Escape Room*, the caged-in mansion of *Abigail*, the fortified house in *Heretic*, or stalked by the monsters as in *Saw* or *The Strangers*.

6. SHELTER IN THE STORM – A snowstorm, flood, or some extreme weather event can cut off characters from the outside world and force them to hunker down in a place of shelter. Examples include *Storm of the Century* and *The Fog*.

7. HOUSE INVADED – The house is mundane, be it an ordinary home, a cabin, or a grocery store, but it's surrounded by monsters or a monster clawing to get inside. Examples include the home surrounded by killers in *The Purge* or *You're Next*. Or the car with the circling rabid dog at the end of *Cujo*.

8. MIND/BODY PRISON – Characters are trapped within their own minds, as in *Jacob's Ladder*, or driven to madness by isolation, like in *The Shining*. They may also be slowly overtaken by horrific forces—biological, like in *The Fly* or *The Substance*, or supernatural, as seen in *The Exorcist* or *The Wolfman*.

9. STRANGE LAND – Being trapped in a foreign country or culture, like in *Hostel* or *The Ruins*, or being trapped in an unfamiliar or hostile culture, like in *The Wicker Man* or *Midsommar* or *Get Out*.

10. SINISTER SUBURBS – Being trapped in a suburban neighborhood or a small town by people who are somehow alien to you, like in *The Stepford Wives*.

11. SOCIAL MAZE – The hero is helpless because the people around them are part of the problem or gaslighting them at every turn. Examples include *Get Out*, *Speak No Evil*, *Rosemary's Baby*, *They Live*, *Hereditary*, and *The Faculty*.

12. EVIL EARTH – There's nowhere to run because the monsters are everywhere. The story becomes more about keeping the monsters out of a small sanctuary. Many zombie movies like *A Quiet Place*, *Dawn of the Dead*, and *Night of the Living Dead* use this technique, as do *I Am Legend* and the Eldritch horror of *The Mist*.

13. EVIL WITHOUT BORDERS – The monster is so relentless it will go anywhere and to any length to hunt the hero, whether it's a town or across the ends of the earth. The horror comes from an unyielding force that pursues the hero, often regardless of time or distance. Examples include *Final Destination* and *It Follows*, where the terror is persistent and unavoidable, or movies like *Terrifier*, *The Invisible Man*, and *The Hitcher*, where a single force pursues its prey without any geographic boundaries and the hero can't escape simply because everywhere they go is a hunting ground.

ATMOSPHERE

When you choose your MITH's house, consider how it can create a sense of dread and unease. Some houses embody the essence of the genre and the history of horror—the old Transylvanian castle, the cabin in the woods, the derelict boat, and a dark and spooky cave all generate certain imprinted memories in horror fans. Even new spins on these tropes—imagine the derelict colony in *Aliens* or Chernobyl in *Chernobyl Diaries*—can give similar dreadful vibes.

Some settings turn the gothic notion of atmosphere on its head, bringing the horror to mundane places we encounter in our daily lives. Like the grocery store in *The Mist*. The suburban home in *Poltergeist*. The commuter train in *Train to Busan*. Or practically every Stephen King book I devoured as a kid.

Certain settings provide additional threats beyond the monster of the story, like the seedy streets in *Hostel*, where dangerous predators lurk in every alley, or the vast ocean in *Open Water*, which provides threats of drowning and hypothermia even before the sharks show up.

Culture, history, and people can play an important part too. The culture clash of people and their lifestyles in *The Wicker Man* and *Midsommar* serve as a ticking time bomb of secrets and danger beneath the surface. *Get Out* places a Black man in a setting surrounded by Southern white people, which provides a subtle yet simmering racial tension—as if the horror is ultimately being served with a fake smile.

Other settings ooze vulnerability. The farmhouse in *A Quiet Place* feels wide open and defenseless. The rundown neighborhood in *Barbarian* is just downright shady. Still, other locations are so remote there's zero chance anyone will ever help, like the ice station in *The Thing* or the distant abandoned Overlook Hotel in *The Shining*.

EXERCISES

1. Focusing on the "trap" in your story, answer the following questions:
   a) Why is there no obvious/easy way for your heroes to escape the horror?
   b) Why is there no obvious/easy way for your heroes to get help?

2. From the list in this chapter, determine your house type (e.g., The Place No One Dares to Go, Shelter in the Storm, etc.).

3. Give your house some atmosphere.
   a) How can the setting create a sense of dread and unease?
   b) What are the history and features of the location that can be unsettling? What cultural or historical elements can add to the horror?
   c) How can the environment itself pose additional threats?
   d) Look at natural dangers like weather, terrain, or isolation. What mundane elements can be twisted to enhance the horror?

4. How does the setting amplify the protagonists' vulnerabilities? Reflect on the characters' personal fears and weaknesses and how the environment exploits them.

CHAPTER 4: THE SIN

The House and the Monster elements are pretty intuitive from the mere name of the genre "Monster in the House." But when I read the original *Save the Cat!* and Blake Snyder mentioned **the sin**, it was a revelation.

Until then, my horror lacked something. I was good at kills and gags and fright and dread but lacked that extra level of meaning and metaphor. Occasionally I'd luck into it. But usually, my horror stories were one dimensional. I was playing checkers while Stephen King and John Carpenter and Wes Craven were playing chess.

The sin adds that extra dimension. It's the special sauce that elevates a horror story from gratuitous thrills to a relevant story with purpose.

There's another more "sinister" function to the MITH's sin. Movies and novels portray life the way we wish it would be, while many horror stories take a dark menacing route. But going back to the E.C. Comics I read as a kid, horror stories are typically morality tales, and they follow the basic "karma equity rules" present in any movie: "In the end, Good is rewarded. Evil is punished."

The sin takes these rules of justice and uses them against us. If our "good guys" are responsible in either a direct or somehow existential way, they're vulnerable. Karmic rules put a target on their backs.

The sin must be atoned for. Even if our hero is presumably innocent of the sin, there's a blood debt to be paid and they're in the crosshairs. While it won't be totally fair if they die, it'll be understandable, perhaps even justified. Which means... uh-oh... our heroes might die.

Believe it or not, the sin is actually what keeps horror from being sinical. (See what I did there? Two sin puns in a chapter! Bonus!) In nihilistic stories, evil just happens, and then you die... too bad! Life stinks. But when the sin is responsible for the bad, there's an understandable logic. A lesson. Some glimmer of hope. Because even if everyone dies, the audience goes away thinking, "Hey, well, at least justice is served and we're safe so long as we don't commit that sin."

TYPES OF SINS

The sin should be a primal one. And for the sin to resonate, it shouldn't be nuanced; the wrongdoing should basically be something we all agree is "bad."

Here's a list of common sins that unleash evil in horror movies, along with some story examples of where you might see them. Use this list to brainstorm the core sin of your story. There are really two things to think of:

1. If you have your monster, what's the metaphor for the real-life terror they represent? What's the reason that real-life horror exists in the world? What are its root causes?
2. Is there some issue or sin you have strong opinions about or that has affected your life? What are two big life problems you have or have had? What sin is at their root cause?

There are likely more sins you can think of or more specific versions of these general ones. Consider these party-starters. Think your own up and add to the list!

1. GREED – In *The Monkey's Paw*, the characters' greed for wishes unleashes a malevolent beast. In the *Wishmaster* movies, the characters' desires for riches lead to disastrous consequences. In *Jaws*, the town's greed for profit overrides public safety, creating a hunting ground for a ravenous shark.

2. GLUTTONY – In *Dead Alive*, the mother's insatiable gluttony transforms her into a zombie, spreading the disease. In *The Stuff*, people's insatiable craving for a dessert-like substance turns them into voracious monsters.

3. LUST – The promiscuous behavior of the main characters in *It Follows* brings about an evil force that pursues them relentlessly. In *Cabin Fever*, sexual encounters lead to the rapid spread of a killer disease.

4. ENVY – In *Wish Upon*, the main character's envy of her high-school peers drives her to use a Wish Box, unknowingly invoking dangerous powers. In *X*, the overt sexuality is really a red herring; envy is the ultimate sin that brings about the monster.

5. PRIDE – In *Carrie*, pride leads to jealousy and ultimately triggers a prank that causes death and destruction at the prom. In *Frailty*, a father's prideful belief in being chosen by God drives him to commit horrific acts.

6. WRATH – Movies like *Last House on the Left*, *Mandy*, and *I Saw the Devil* depict characters embarking on murderous rampages, awakening the monster within them and exposing them to unimaginable horrors.

7. SLOTH – In *Idle Hands*, the main character's lack of ambition and complacency becomes an invitation for evil to take hold. In *Shaun of the Dead*, the main characters are so aimless and narcissistic, they barely recognize a zombie apocalypse is taking shape around them.

8. HUBRIS/ARROGANCE – The amateur documentary team's arrogance and overconfidence in *The Blair Witch Project* lead them into the haunted woods, where they face terrifying supernatural forces. Similarly, in *1408*, a skeptical reporter's hubris drives him to enter one of the most haunted places without fear or caution, unleashing the evil within. In *Don't Breathe*, privileged arrogance brings about the monster when rich people try to live above the law and, ultimately, their actions lead to the monster's need for justice.

9. SELFISHNESS/NARCISSISM – In *Drag Me to Hell*, a woman prioritizes her own desires for promotion over the livelihood of a desperate old woman, resulting in a curse that threatens her very soul.

10. VANITY – Works like *Death Becomes Her, The Substance,* and *A Picture of Dorian Gray* explore the consequences of excessive vanity, where individuals' obsession with their appearance or self-image leads to disturbing and horrifying outcomes.

11. DECEIT – In *Audition*, the hero's fake audition brings him into contact with the monster. In *I Know What You Did Last Summer*, the group's coverup leads to their terror.

12. BETRAYAL – *The Thing* showcases how paranoia fuels the characters' betrayal of each other, leading to escalating horror.

13. SACRILEGE – Movies like *The Exorcist* and *The Nun* explore the consequences of disrespecting religious boundaries and beliefs. In *Pet Sematary*, the main characters disrespect the dead by burying them in an unhallowed burial ground, triggering a chain of supernatural events. The characters' disregard for sacred objects or rituals inadvertently invites malevolent entities, leading to terrifying and supernatural encounters.

14. CURIOSITY – The *Evil Dead* and *The Conjuring* films show how characters' curiosity about the paranormal leads them to uncover dark and malevolent forces. Their relentless pursuit of the truth exposes them to unimaginable horrors that threaten their sanity and lives.

15. TRESPASSING – *The Chernobyl Diaries* revolves around a group of characters who trespass into the forbidden area of the abandoned city of Chernobyl, only to encounter horrifying creatures and face a fight for their lives.

16. RECKLESSNESS – In *The Shallows*, a surfer's recklessness leads her to a secluded beach with a menacing monster of a shark. In *Hostel*, backpackers are lured into some dangerous streets of Slovakia.

17. COMPLACENCY – In *Get Out*, a world of letting subtle racist infractions slide leads to a dangerous monster working in the shadows, preying on African Americans for their own selfish reasons. Sometimes not speaking up is a sin itself.

18. PAST CRUELTIES OR INJUSTICE – In movies like *Friday the 13th* or *A Nightmare on Elm Street* or *The Ring*, historical injustices or unresolved past actions lead to supernatural retribution or horror. The sins of the past (even if sometimes justified, and often involving neglect, abuse, or violent acts) manifest in the present as supernatural or monstrous consequences.

THE SIN CONNECTS WITH THE MONSTER

The sin is a past event that connects to the current events of the story. There are four ways this usually happens:

1. THE SIN SUMMONS THE MONSTER – Monsters are often from different worlds. Sometimes the sin brings them into our world or awakens them in some way: playing with the puzzle box in *Hellraiser*, reckless testing of atomic weapons in *Godzilla*, or the hubris of reading the Necronomicon in *Evil Dead*.

2. THE SIN CREATES THE MONSTER – Often through a horrendous act, the monster is created as a vehicle of vengeance or justice. In these cases, the monster serves as a karmic punishment to the perpetrated sins. Freddy Krueger, Jason Voorhees, and many other slasher villains are creatures of vengeance. Some monsters are created by the sins of science crossing into godly territory, as in *The Fly* or *Frankenstein* or *Re-Animator*.

3. THE SIN PUSHES THE HERO INTO THE WORLD OF THE MONSTER – Whether it's the thieves entering the monster's lair in *Don't Breathe* or vacationers going where they shouldn't in *The Ruins* or *Hostel*, treading into places either physical or ideological can force encounters with monsters.

4. THE SIN ALLOWS THE MONSTER TO THRIVE – In some stories, secrets and not confronting evil or the past bring about the monster. *It* and *Candyman* show ongoing evil that festers through the sin of complacency or the fear of confronting evils in the world.

DOES THE SIN SHAPE YOUR STORY'S THEME OR CHARACTER ARC?

Usually. Not always. But usually. The sin of your story is often thematic and commonly related to the metaphor of the monster mentioned in the Lore section in the previous chapter. But it's not always the flaw your main character is dealing with. For example, the sin of your movie might be "playing with science without ethics is bad," but your main character might not even be interested in science. In some cases, the sin and the lessons the character needs to learn are out of sync.

Even in these cases, you can often find common ground between the sin and the arc. What's the "note behind the note" of your sin (or the larger sin behind the specific one that brings about the monster)? Try to find a personal flaw that leads to someone committing such a sin. Why are the bad guys trying to use science without ethics? Maybe greed or ego or maybe their bosses are forcing them and they're afraid to speak up. Maybe they're drowning in self-doubt and willing to cut corners to prove to the world they're worthy.

Relatable human dilemmas are the stuff of theme and character arcs. So, your main character might suffer a similar dilemma that has nothing to do with science but is the same lesson that if that mad scientist had learned, the world would be a better (or at least safer) place.

EXERCISES

In your story:

1. What's the sin that brings about the monster?
2. What type of character flaw might be present in someone who commits this sin?
3. If the hero is not the one committing the sin that brings about the monster, how does this character flaw relate to your hero's own character flaw? What can your hero learn about their own flaw from the sin that brought about the monster?
4. How do you relate to the sin? Has it affected your life in a personal or existential way? How can this inform your story or your characters? In short, why are *you* the person to write this story?

CHAPTER 5: SCARE POTENTIAL

You have the monster, the house, the sin... but what's scary about your story? Thinking about what scares people and extrapolating that to the monster or the house is a good start. Here are some common fears:

1. FEAR OF SPIDERS (ARACHNOPHOBIA) – Horror films like *Eight-Legged Freaks* and *Big Ass Spider* deliver giant mutant arachnids.

2. FEAR OF SNAKES (OPHIDIOPHOBIA) – *Anaconda* follows a documentary crew that encounters a monstrous snake in the Amazon rainforest, triggering their worst fears.

3. FEAR OF ENCLOSED SPACES (CLAUSTROPHOBIA) – *Buried* is about a man trapped in a coffin. *The Descent* features a group of women trapped in a cave system, where they not only battle creatures but also their own claustrophobic fears.

4. FEAR OF HEIGHTS (ACROPHOBIA) – *Vertical Limit* and *Fall* trap heroes in high-altitude battles of survival.

5. FEAR OF THE DARK (NYCTOPHOBIA) – *Lights Out* explores the terror of a malevolent entity that can only be seen in the dark, exploiting the fear of darkness and the unknown.

6. FEAR OF THE UNKNOWN (XENOPHOBIA) – The classic film *Alien* preys on the fear of the unknown as a space crew encounters a deadly extraterrestrial organism on a distant planet.

7. FEAR OF THE SUPERNATURAL (CACOPHOBIA) – *The Conjuring* series capitalizes on the fear of the supernatural, depicting real-life paranormal investigators confronting malevolent spirits.

8. FEAR OF ABANDONMENT (AUTOPHOBIA) – In *The Others*, a woman believes her house is haunted, triggering her fear of abandonment as she navigates a haunting mystery.

9. FEAR OF ISOLATION (ISOLOPHOBIA) – *The Shining* amplifies the fear of isolation as a writer and his family are snowed in at a remote hotel, leading to psychological unraveling.

10. FEAR OF THE UNSEEN (PARANOIA) – *The Babadook* symbolizes a mother's descent into madness and paranoia as she believes a malevolent entity is haunting her and her son.

11. FEAR OF LOSS OF IDENTITY (DISSOCIATIVE IDENTITY) – Possession movies like *The Exorcist* show people slowly losing themselves to demonic entities.

12. FEAR OF DEATH (THANATOPHOBIA) – In *Final Destination*, death literally pursues the heroes in gruesome and unexpected ways.

13. FEAR OF GERMS OR DIRT (MYSOPHOBIA) – In *Cabin Fever*, fear of infection from a flesh-eating virus takes center stage.

14. FEAR OF OTHERS (SOCIAL PHOBIA) – A movie like *Carrie* portrays social phobia with tragic supernatural consequences.

It's important to know what scares others... but screenplays are about *you*. You need to figure out why this story would scare the crap out of you. If it scares you, it'll scare others.

When I was jumping out at people from behind that tree, the truth was... I HATED to be jump scared. I hated to walk through that dark woods all alone. I knew that what scared me would scare other people.

WHAT SCARES YOU?

To help, here's a massive list. If you don't mind ruining the book... highlight or circle some of your fears. Or you can save the book by writing your faves on a sticky note or something.

Abduction
Alligators
Amputation
Authority
Balloons popping
Barriers
Bed bugs
Beheading
Betrayal
Birds (large, aggressive)
Black holes
Black magic
Blood transfusions
Boarding school
Boats
Body odor
Bones breaking
Brain injuries
Breathing difficulties
Bridges collapsing
Bugs crawling in ears
Burglary
Cannibalism
Carbon monoxide poisoning
Cardiac arrest
Carnivals
Catastrophic events
Chemical spills
Choking
Claustrophobia
Cockroaches
Coffins
Cold temperatures
Confrontation
Contamination
Controlling behavior
Cults
Curses
Cyberbullying
Dams breaking
Darkness (fear of the dark)
Decapitation
Deformities
Dental equipment
Detention
Disasters
Disease outbreaks
Disfigurement
Diving
Doctors
Drowning
Drugs
Dust
Earthquakes
Eclipses
Electrocution
Elevators
Enclosed spaces
End of the world
Eternal damnation
Explosions
Eye injuries
Fainting
Failure (fear of failure)
Famine
Feral animals
Ferris wheels
Fevers
Filing cabinets
Fire drills
Fireworks
Fish hooks
Floods
Flying insects
Fog
Forest fires
Fortune tellers
Fossils

Freezing to death
Fungi
Funeral homes
Gallows
Garbage dumps
Gas leaks
Genetic disorders
Ghost ships
Gigantic waves
Glaciers
Glass shards
Global warming
Glue traps
Goats
Graveyards
Guillotines
Gunshots
Hangings
Haunted houses
Heatstroke
Helicopters
Heliophobia (fear of the sea)
Hell
High places
Holes
Hoarding
Hostages
Hurricanes
Hypothermia
Icebergs
Identity theft
Impalement
Injections
Insanity
Invasive medical procedures
Jail
Jealousy
Jellyfish stings
Jet engines failing
Jumping from heights
Kidnapping
Killer bees
Knives
Ladders
Lakes
Landfills
Landmines
Lice
Lightning strikes
Limb amputation
Lizards
Locks (being trapped)
Losing a sense (sight, hearing, etc.)
Machinery malfunctions
Maggots
Malnutrition
Mannequins
Marsupials
Masturbation (fear of)
Medical errors
Medieval torture devices
Meltdowns
Mercury poisoning
Meteors
Mice
Military conflict
Mineshafts collapsing
Mistreatment
Mold
Moths
Mountain climbing
Mudslides
Murder
Murderers
Mushrooms
Narrow spaces
Natural disasters
Needle phobia
Neglect
Negligence

Nightmares
Noise
Nuclear accidents
Nuclear war
Nudity
Obsessive-compulsive disorder (fear of)
Ocean waves
Odors
Offending others
Ostracism
Overpopulation
Oxygen deprivation
Panic attacks
Parasites
Parasitic worms
Peacocks
Penetration
People in costumes
Persecution
Pesticides
Phobias
Physical pain
Pigeons
Pirates
Plagues
Planes crashing
Plastic surgery
Pollution
Possession
Post-apocalyptic scenarios
Poverty
Prejudice
Pressure
Priests
Protests
Psychiatric hospitals
Psychopaths
Public speaking
Pyromania
Quicksand
Rabies
Radiation
Razor blades
Rejection
Religion
Relapse
Rats
Religion
Renunciation
Resurrection
Retirement
Reptiles
Respiratory diseases
Responsibility
Resuscitation
Retaliation
Retirement homes
Riding in cars
Riding in elevators
Rituals
Road rage
Rocks falling
Rodents
Rotting flesh
Royalty
Running out of resources
Sabotage
Sacrifice
Sailing
Sanitation
Satanic rituals
Schizophrenia
School shootings
Scorpions
Scurvy
Sea creatures
Seals (animal)
Seasons changing
Self-sacrifice

Selfishness
Self-reliance
Serpents
Sewage
Sexuality
Shackles
Shaming
Sharing
Sharks
Shipwrecks
Shopping malls
Shotgun weddings
Shyness
Sickness
Sirens
Skeletons
Skin diseases
Skin lesions
Skunks
Slavery
Slaughterhouses
Slime
Sloths
Smog
Smothering
Snails
Snares
Snipers
Snow
Social situations
Socialism
Solitude
Sound
Spiders
Spirits
Spontaneous combustion
Spores
Spyware
Squids
Squirrels
Starvation
STDs
Stings
Stomach ailments
Stomach-turning sights
Storms
Strangulation
Strangers
Strawberries
Stuttering
Suffocation
Suicide
Supernatural beings
Surgery
Surprises
Survival
Swamps
Swarms
Swimming
Swords
Symbolism
Seduction
Seizures
Self-destruction
Self-harm
Self-mutilation
Syringes
Taboos
Taking tests
Tarantulas
Tattoos
Taxidermy
Technology
Teenagers
Teeth
Telephones
Temptation
Terrorism
Testicles
Tetanus

Theft
Time running out
Tornadoes
Torture
Toxic substances
Traitors
Trains
Trapped
Trash
Traveling alone
Trees falling
Tremors
Trust issues
Tsunamis
Tunnels
Tyranny
Uncertainty
Uncontrollable urges
Underachievement
Undercooked food
Underground spaces
Unemployment
Unfamiliar environments
Unfamiliar situations
Unknown
Unknown (fear of)
Unpredictability
Unrest
Unstable structures
Unwanted advances
Upsetting news
Urban legends
Urinals
Urns
Vaccinations
Vampires
Venomous creatures
Vermin
Vices
Victims
Violence
Viral outbreaks
Viruses
Volcanoes
Vomiting
Voyeurism
Walking alone at night
Wasps
Water pollution
Waterborne illnesses
Wax figures
Weakness
Weather phenomena
Weight gain
Weight loss
Wells
Werewolves
Witches
Witchcraft
Wolf attacks
Wolves
Worms
Wounds
Wrinkles
Wrong decisions
Xenophobia (fear of dryness)
Xylophobia (fear of forests)
Yellow fever
Yelling
Yeti
Yin yang symbols
Yuletide
Zebra crossings
Zebras
Zenophobia (fear of religion)
Zits
Zoos
Zombification
Zombies

Look at what you circled. Do any of these relate to your story? Do any of them relate directly to what's scary about your monster or your house, pushing against these fears? If they do, jackpot! Lean into those hard!

If not, see if there's a place to adjust the Monster in the House elements or the characters to lean into what truly scares *you*. Your own fears make excellent roadmaps for the scarefest you're designing. Use 'em. How do they relate to the monster's method of attack or the monster's metaphor or the house or the method of isolation?

The goal when writing is to creep yourself out, poke at the edges of what makes you uncomfortable. Then poke harder. If you get a little scared or feel a little queasy or need to sleep with the lights on... you know you're doing it right.

EXERCISES

1. Circle all of your fears in the list in this chapter.
2. Review your fears. Do any of them relate to either the monster or the house of the story you're developing?
3. Can you incorporate your fears into the monster or the house of the story you're developing?

CHAPTER 6: BUT HORROR HAS NO BOUNDS... RIGHT?

One of the reasons horror is so much fun is because it has no guardrails. It's a rollercoaster without a safety bar.

Horror is wild, anarchic, and UNRULY... right?

Well, yes and no.

Let's start with the "no."

Save the Cat! sometimes gets grief for being formulaic and predictable. "*There are no rules!*" shout its critics.

Dudes, I come from horror movies. Go watch some of my twisted stuff. Or watch some of the stuff I love. I'm one of the weirdos. I'm UNRULY!!! My writing thrives on the unpredictable. It revels in shock (and schlock!). For some of my more grim and realistic work, I need to stay clear of anything that feels artificial or stylized or movie-ish so the audience doesn't ever feel too safe or doesn't sense the world they're seeing in the story is different from the real world. I work overtime to make you forget that "it's just a movie."

Take it from a fellow horror freak, the things old-school *Save the Cat!* does best (story structure and transformational arc) do not stifle your ability to scare the bejesus out of people. In fact, *STC!* takes away some of the guesswork when it comes to crafting a strong story, so you can focus on character and terror and crafting the primal nightmares we all can't wait to see.

Many of my favorite horror movies and novels follow the traditional *Save the Cat!* beats. *The Exorcist*, *Jaws*, *Halloween*, *The Shining*, *Aliens*, *Shaun of the Dead*, *Dawn of the Dead*, *A Nightmare on Elm Street*, *Get Out*, *Pet Sematary*, *Scream*, *The Blair Witch Project* are all traditional, well-told Monster in the House stories that follow *Save the Cat!*, but you never notice or care because the tension is off the charts and the frights are relentless.

Now, let's talk the "yes" part.

Yes, horror breaks the rules. One of the best ways to scare someone is to take them down a familiar path, a seemingly safe one, and make a sudden turn into terror territory. *Save the Cat!* helps with that too. You can be more deliberate in your storytelling and manipulate your audience into thinking they know what's about to happen, and then pull the rug out from under them and hurl them straight into terror territory.

But still, there are storytelling "rules" that must be followed:

- All movies need a happy ending, right? Bah! Check out *The Mist*!
- Villains always lose. Evil must be vanquished. Well, tell that to Freddy Kreuger or Michael Myers.
- What about the old "they wouldn't kill a kid" rule? Meh. Check out *Pet Sematary* and *It*. Stephen King is very, very cruel. That's why we love him.
- But those are just side characters. Main characters are safe, right? You can't kill them off. The movie would just suddenly end. Two words for you: shower scene!
- Assuming the heroes survive, those main characters learn a lesson and become better people. Well, sometimes they become the monster and terrorize the people they love, like in *The Shining* and *The Fly*.

These classic moments of shock aren't so impactful because they ignore all audience expectations and storytelling practices in some creative anarchy of no restraints; they work because the writers know what the audience is thinking and they're toying with them. These writers know how to make us feel safe and they also know there are places they're not supposed to go. They lure us into a false sense of security and then they go there, to the dark forbidden place.

Horror breaks the mold in other ways, too. It frequently pushes the envelope of taste by taking gore and violence into uncomfortable territory. On occasion, it can present situations that are triggering and sometimes downright offensive. It can get trippy and surreal. It can end abruptly and shockingly. And more often than not, it has down endings.

Horror stories can also be ambiguous. Monsters are often hidden in the shadows, sometimes only glimpsed (like *Jaws*), sometimes never even seen (like *The Blair Witch Project*). The evil is often not understood or explained—sometimes it operates without a plan or a purpose; sometimes it doesn't make any sense at all.

This ambiguity can be frustrating to creatives who aren't immersed in horror and like their story logic tied in a tight bow, but this sense of the unexplainable is part of the fabric of horror. It's part of what makes horror scary. This lack of clear answers mirrors real-life fears. When terrifying things happen, we often struggle to make sense of them, and part of what turns them into nightmares is that we can never fully understand or explain them.

It's this mix of understanding audience expectations but also knowing what makes horror work that is the reason I wanted to write this book. Because in the end, a great horror story is a devilish mixture of both. The best horror stories are 90-95% classic storytelling and about 5-10% madness. You, the writer, get to choose where to bring the madness.

PART 2: YOUR HIGH-LEVEL HORROR STORY

CHAPTER 7: STORY DNA

Story in essence is "something unusual happening to someone." It's not about the ordinary. In terms of story, we're not referring to the hero's familiar, everyday world—the "ordinary world" where life feels stable and predictable. Instead, we're talking about the "upside-down worlds," where the rules are distorted, normalcy is disrupted, and everything is thrown into chaos.

Let me tell you about the time I spent the night in a haunted house.

Let me tell you about the time I had a dream that seemed to become true and no one believed me.

Let me tell you about the time a scary clown chased me.

In a MITH story, **the ordinary world vs. the upside-down world** is most often represented by the before and after picture of when the monster is part of your hero's life.

Life before the hero feeds Gizmo food after midnight vs. the upside-down world with the Gremlins.

Life before Jack Torrance takes the caretaker job at the Overlook Hotel vs. the upside-down world where the hotel drives him to madness and attempted murder.

Life before Laurie Strode crosses paths with Michael Myers on Halloween night vs. the upside-down world where a masked killer relentlessly hunts her.

Life before the Lutz family moves into their dream home in Amityville vs. the upside-down world where the house turns into a psychological and supernatural nightmare.

Life before little Regan is possessed vs. the upside-down world where she's cussing and vomiting pea-soup and levitating over the bed.

The engine of story is a big dramatic question about the outcome of this upside-down world: Will the hero win or will they lose and suffer the horrible consequences?

Will I survive my night in the haunted house?

Can I convince my friends my dream is a premonition or will my nightmare come true?

Will I be able to outrun the scary clown or will I suffer a horrible demise?

Turns out the basics of every story is found by answering four simple questions about this upside-down world of your story:

1) Who is the Hero?

Choose an intriguing protagonist for your horror story, someone whom audiences will root for and empathize with. Oh, and don't be fooled by the word "hero." The hero of your story might be despicable. They might be a con man or a crook or a liar or a cheat. Whoever they are, they're the primary focus of our attention.

2) What is their Goal?

Determine what your protagonist desires or seeks to achieve. This goal should be specific and meaningful, driving the story forward.

3) What's the Obstacle in the way?

Create a formidable obstacle that stands in the way of your hero's goal. This could be a malevolent entity, a supernatural force, a monstrous creature, or even a psychological threat.

4) What's at Stake if they fail?

Clearly outline what will happen if the hero fails to achieve their goal. The stakes should be high and carry significant consequences, keeping the tension and suspense at a peak. Really, they should be Life or Death.

Before diving any deeper into your plot, figure these four questions out. And as an added bonus, these same elements of Story DNA also lay the foundation for a great logline. A strong logline can be created by inserting the DNA into a **basic logline template**:

After a (Unexpected Event), a (Hero) must overcome (Obstacle) to achieve (Goal) or else (Stakes).

Here are two examples of horror loglines using this approach:

***The Conjuring* logline**

After a family moves into a remote farmhouse (unexpected event), a pair of paranormal investigators (heroes) must confront the vengeful spirit haunting the property (obstacle) before it destroys them and claims their souls (stakes).

Get Out logline

After accepting an invitation to visit his girlfriend's family estate (unexpected event), a young African-American man (hero) must uncover the horrifying truth behind the seemingly idyllic facade (obstacle) before he becomes the next victim of a sinister conspiracy (stakes).

It's crucial to establish your Story DNA and logline before diving into story development. The Story DNA serves as the spine of your narrative—the central thread that holds everything together. Without defining it upfront, you risk building a story that feels disjointed, aimless, or structurally unsound.

EXERCISES

1. List a few of your favorite horror movies or books. Who is the hero? What's their goal? What's in the way? Why do they have to act right now, with no delay and no excuses?
2. For your own story idea, write down the hero, goal, obstacle, and stakes.
3. For those same ideas, write a logline that clearly communicates the hero, goal, obstacle, and stakes.

ONE NOTE: If you find these exercises impossible for a particular favorite or your own idea, it might be that you're dealing with a slow burn horror story. We'll discuss slow burn horror later, and you can revisit this exercise then.

CHAPTER 8: WHAT STORY ARE YOU TELLING?

Okay, you've done a ton of pre-writing prep. You know your monster and the house and even the deeper themes and the metaphors your story is about. You even have a handle on what's scary about your story and why it personally terrifies you.

Before we jump into turning this thing into a full-blown story, I'd like you to get one more clarification. I'd like you to ask yourself, "What kind of story are you telling?"

"Monster in the House, right?" is probably your answer.

Good. Good. We're 80% there. But under the banner of Monster in the House, there are a few common paths stories take. These Monster in the House **subgenres** can help you narrow down the story you are telling. More importantly, they can provide clues as to certain directions or sub-beats that might appear in the story.

Have a look below and see if you can find a subgenre for your story:

MONSTER IN THE HOUSE SUBGENRES

1. MONSTER BUDDY – The hero has a monster as a friend or a confidant, someone who is looking out for them in a monstrous way. As the monster's "good deeds" escalate, the hero battles to stop them. The story becomes a battle for survival. Examples include *M3GAN*, *King Kong*, *The Phantom of the Opera*.

Elements of a Monster Buddy:

- Misunderstood Monster – The monster forms an unusual bond with the hero, leading to a friendship/love/obsession that pushes boundaries. The monster usually has a heart... and not just one in a jar.
- Monster Knows Best – The monster often secretly helps the hero in horrific ways.
- Moral Dilemma – As the monster's actions escalate, the hero is torn between protecting their friend and stopping the destructive path.

2. I'M THE MONSTER – The hero, through disease, curse, possession, or mental affliction, becomes a monster. The horror comes from their lack of control over their impulses or their inability to judge right from wrong. Examples of this type of horror story include *The Shining, The Fly, American Psycho, May, The Wolfman*.

Elements of I'm the Monster:

- Internal Struggle – The hero battles their inner demons, struggling to control their monstrous impulses or powers.
- Isolation and Paranoia – The hero becomes isolated from others, fearing that they will be rejected or hunted down for what they have become.
- Hero Goes Full-Monster – Usually in Act 3, the hero goes full-monster and there's a protagonist switch where a B-Story character or someone the hero loves becomes the hero battling the beast.

3. KEEP THEM OUT – The monsters are trying to invade a "safe place": a bunker, a panic room, a cabin in the woods, or a locked house. The monsters may be kept out or actually invade. Examples of this subgenre include *Dawn of the Dead, You're Next, The Purge, Greenroom*.

Elements of a Keep Them Out:

- Claustrophobia – The story is filled with suspense as the heroes barricade themselves in a safe place, constantly facing the threat of invasion.
- MacGyver Survivor – The heroes must rely on their ingenuity and limited resources to defend themselves against the relentless onslaught of monsters.
- Group Dynamics – The interactions and conflicts among the characters in the safe place can add depth to the story, as they must work together to survive.

4. ESCAPE THE LAIR – The hero is trapped in the monster's lair and must survive and escape. Examples of this type of horror story include *The Blair Witch Project, The Descent, Heretic, Don't Breathe*.

Elements of Escape the Lair:

- Survival Instincts – The hero must tap into their survival instincts, using their wits and courage to outsmart the monster and escape.
- Unraveling the Mystery – The lair may hold clues or secrets that the hero must uncover to understand the monster's origins or weaknesses.

5. STRANGER IN A STRANGE LAND – This subgenre is akin to a slow burn version of "Escape the Lair." Our hero finds themselves as a stranger in a strange land, sensing that something is wrong. However, everyone around them appears either unconcerned or ignorant of the warning signs—likely because they are either in league with the monsters or are the monsters themselves. Examples include *Midsommar*, *Get Out*, *Rosemary's Baby*, *Hostel.*

Elements of Stranger in a Strange Land:

- A Group – An institution, society, or community that is visited by the hero and is in league with the monster or is in fact the monster.
- Warning Signs & Gaslighting – The second act of these stories usually is filled with red flags and lots of gaslighting.

6. LAST SURVIVOR STANDING – A relentless, unstoppable monster is coming for a group of heroes. They must solve a mystery (who's the killer?) or find a way to slay the monster to survive. Examples include *Scream*, *Halloween*, *Friday the 13th*.

Elements of Last Survivor Standing:

- Final Girl/Boy – The lone survivor must face off against the relentless monster, becoming the embodiment of survival and resilience.
- Who's the Monster? – The story may involve misdirection and clues that keep both the characters and the audience guessing about the monster's identity.
- Mano-Y-Monster – The ultimate confrontation between the hero and the monster is a pivotal and suspenseful moment that determines the hero's fate.

7. WHAT THE CURSE?! – The hero or group of heroes must deal with a curse or an outbreak that threatens their lives or the lives of someone they love. Examples include *The Exorcist*, *The Ring*, *It Follows*, *Cabin in the Woods*.

Elements of What the Curse?!:

- Dead by Dawn – The urgency to find a solution intensifies as the curse or outbreak spreads, leaving little time for mistakes. Winning the day usually involves finding a cure or unraveling a mystery that will lead to a solution.

- Dark Dilemma – The heroes are forced to make painful decisions to protect others or end the curse, often with personal sacrifices.

8. HUNT A KILLER – A hero is tasked with hunting down a killer before it kills again. With every step closer, the body count increases, and the hero becomes more personally affected by the killings. Examples: *Jaws*, *Nope*, *Se7en*, *Silence of the Lambs*

Elements of Hunt a Killer:

- Follow the Clues – The hero embarks on a suspenseful investigation, trying to unravel the killer's motives and identity.
- Rising Body Count – The body count increases as the hero gets closer to the truth, raising the tension and the danger.
- Psychological Toll – The hero's obsession with catching the killer takes a toll on their mental and emotional well-being.

9. SOLVE THE PUZZLE – The only way to beat the killer is to solve a mystery or a puzzle about the monster's origin or motives. Examples include *The Ring*, *The Conjuring*, *Saw*.

Elements of Solve the Puzzle:

- Evil Enigma – The hero must delve into the mysterious origins of the monster, facing supernatural elements to uncover the truth.
- Cryptic Clues – The story may involve cryptic clues or symbols that the hero must decipher to understand the monster's weaknesses or motivations.
- Uncovering Dark Secrets – Solving the puzzle leads to unsettling revelations (sometimes about the hero!), exposing hidden secrets that add depth to the horror.

As always, these subgenres can be combined. For example, a curse movie like *The Ring* might also have a mystery to be solved.

Tone-O-Meter

Okay, pop quiz, have you seen the movie about the young boy who is home alone and fends off invaders using improvised weapons within their house?

No, not *Home Alone*, the one with a similar premise but drastically different tone. It's called *The Aggression Scale*. It's about a disturbed teenager who uses his cunning and resourcefulness to set deadly traps and fight back against ruthless hitmen invading his home. This film is filled with brutal, realistic violence and creates a chilling atmosphere, exploring themes of survival and psychological trauma.

With a slight tweak of tone, everything changes.

While horror is built to terrify, there are many levels of fright, from the hilarious scares of *Shaun of the Dead* to the spine-chilling realism of *The Blair Witch Project*.

Tone is all about the vibe you want to create and the feelings you want to stir. Do you want a stylized and somewhat artificial world where people are fun and pretty, the dialogue is quippy, and the settings are idealistic? Or are you aiming for that gritty "is this even real?" vibe? Or something in between?

Take *Scream*, for example. It delivers scares and laughs and is a good time at the movies but it isn't a story that leaves us worried that "this could happen to me." Then you've got *Paranormal Activity* messing with your head, making you forget it's all make-believe. Or a movie like the original *Halloween*, that might make us do a double-take when encountering that creepy quiet adult in a mask on Halloween night.

The Tone-O-Meter is a scale that helps you stay on the right track. It's like finding your movie's soulmate in terms of tone. Let's say we're talking horror movies set in the creepy woods. Here's a little scale for you. (Note: you don't have to fill out the entire scale, just enough to know where you rank):

1 – *Attack of the Killer Tomatoes*: Pure camp and silliness. Killer tomatoes... enough said.

2– *Toxic Avenger* or *Killer Klowns from Outer Space*: Absurd and bizarre, mixing outrageous horror elements with a cartoonish sense of humor.

3 – *Tucker & Dale vs. Evil*: It's like horror and comedy had a weird, hilarious baby.

4 – *Cabin in the Woods*: A wicked fun time with a side of scares.

5 – *Evil Dead 2*: A mix of over-the-top horror and dark humor.

6 – *Cabin Fever*: Getting more serious but over the top enough to still have some laughs.

7 – *Honeymoon*: Creeping toward realism but maintaining an eerie, surreal atmosphere, blending intimate relationship dynamics with unsettling horror elements.

8 – *The Ritual*: Things get seriously intense, but there's room for some unexpected surprises.

9 – *The Blair Witch Project*: Classic, found-footage horror that'll make you question every rustling leaf but is also made to make you think, is it real?

10– *Henry: Portrait of a Serial Killer*: Unflinchingly dark and disturbingly realistic, this film offers a chilling portrayal of a serial killer.

The Tone-O-Meter is your trusty guide. It keeps your scares in check, your laughs on point, and your readers hooked.

Here's one for zombie horror...

1 – *Shaun of the Dead*
2 – *Zombieland*
3 – *Return of the Living Dead*
4 – *Dead Alive*
5 – *Dawn of the Dead*
6 – *Train to Busan*
7 – *28 Days Later*
8 – *World War Z*
9 – *Night of the Living Dead*
10 – *The Walking Dead*

Positioning your own zombie story on this scale will help you zero in on the specific flavor of humor, gore, suspense, or drama in your tale. If nothing else, find at least one tonally comparable story to your own. Decide if your horror story is quippy and meta like *Scream*, brutally serious like *The Texas Chainsaw Massacre*, or splat-stick goofiness like *Evil Dead 2*.

EXERCISES

1. Again, pick some of your favorite horror movies and books— what MITH subgenres are they?
2. For your own story, what MITH subgenre does it best fit?
3. Create a Tone-O-Meter of comparable stories to your own and decide where on the meter your story fits.
4. Now that you have a clearer understanding of the story you're telling, revise your logline. Keep reworking your logline at every step!

PART 3: MONSTER FODDER: HORROR MOVIE HEROES AND CHARACTERS

CHAPTER 9: WHAT'S THE HUMAN DRAMA THAT GETS INTERRUPTED BY THE BIG BAD MONSTER?

Blumhouse head honcho, Jason Blum, once said that the reason some of his biggest horror hits work is because they'd work *without* the scary stuff. On the flip side, most horror stories that fall a little flat are hyper-focused on the monsters and shocks and ooga-booga moments. The characters exist to service the scares or ramp up the body count but we don't care about 'em. There's no human connection. When these underdeveloped characters die or are put in danger, it's less emotional and more technical, and they don't have a journey other than "run, hide, survive."

I was raised on a steady diet of 70s and 80s horror. The movies I rented back then were banking on the spectacle of blood and guts. These flicks were sold on boobs, beast, and blood. VHS pushed the envelope, showing things that were borderline distasteful and a little nasty. Back then, having Bikini Camp Counselor #3 get chased by a dude with a mask and a machete was enough. It was all about the kills. All about the effects.

Sure, there were many movies that bucked the system by delivering franchise-worthy heroes or villains. But many of the ones that went down as classics told deeper stories about the world and humanity and the characters within them. *The Exorcist*, *Rosemary's Baby*, *The Shining*, *Jacob's Ladder*, *Nightmare on Elm Street*, *Candyman*, *Carrie*, *Jaws* all had carefully crafted characters with timely relatable problems that suddenly get interrupted by a Big Bad something-something.

Since horror has bled its way into the mainstream, the word "elevated" gets tossed around. I don't love the term "elevated horror." I think all writing—be it horror or not—should be elevated. The first time I heard the term was when the movie *Taken* came out. Creative execs told me they'd do action if it was "elevated" (meaning like *Taken*). The best I could tell was that "elevated" meant it was a genre movie that "had a big star in it."

There's something to learn there: write a genre movie that could attract a big star. Movie stars are on the lookout for three-dimensional characters that are more than just monster fodder and stories that go beyond the surface and have something to say about our times and the human experience.

The way to deliver elevated horror is to care about your characters as much as you care about your monsters.

But here's what all of us horror freaks know: elevated horror isn't new; it's been around since Bram Stoker and Mary Shelley and Shirley Jackson and Stephen King.

So how do we make sure our characters are more than Monster Snacks? We listen to Jason Blum and create a dramatic story that would be compelling even if the monsters never showed up. That starts with characters.

HORROR CHARACTERS

Evil Dead creator Sam Raimi once stated his three rules of horror:

1 – The innocent must suffer.

2 – The guilty must be punished.

3 – The hero must taste blood to be a man.

While his first two rules have been covered in Chapter 4 (the sin creates a karma-debt that must be paid), it's the third that's vital to forging your heroes. In its essence, horror is about characters going through a bloody rite of passage to learn an important truth. After this frightful endeavor, the character will change. They'll get blood on their hands. They'll find something in themselves they didn't think they had... and live differently forever after. The hero will discover the warrior within, the survivor, the resilient self that doesn't need to ask for help or take orders. They'll learn this by a trial of fire. By tasting blood.

Change means there's something your hero needs to learn. There are three key elements to every good horror hero:

1) A **Flaw** – A personal problem that needs fixing. Example: In the movie *The Shining*, Jack Torrance suffers from alcoholism and a history of violence, which makes him vulnerable to the malevolent spirits that possess the haunted Overlook Hotel.

2) A **Want** –The thing their flawed mind thinks will make them happy. Example: Jack Torrance thinks if he can write his latest novel, all the problems will go away. He thinks everything else is a distraction.

3) A **Need** – The lesson they need to learn to fix the flaw. Example: Jack needs to learn that his own destructive behaviors are the root of his problems in his life and his career. It's not others who are causing the distractions. He might survive if he'd only realize this and stop blaming others.

These three elements define your hero's **internal transformation**, which should reflect a larger thematic concept in your horror screenplay. Once you establish these three transformational elements, you can use it to inform your character choices, particularly their flaws.

Flaws bring depth and humanity to your characters. Characters without flaws can feel cold and distant, while those with imperfections have layers that resonate with the audience. To understand your character's flaw, consider their **shard of glass**—their origin story, usually some personal trauma, that shapes their imperfections. This shard lies deep within the character and must be consciously confronted to initiate healing.

The hero's *want* is the external goal they believe will fix their problems, but often the want leads them astray. However, the hero's true *need*, the lesson they must learn to overcome their flaw, is the core of their character development. The need ties back to your central theme.

In horror, there's one other trait I like to consider: what's their **vulnerability**? Why is this hero most tortured by this particular monster?

The vulnerability is sometimes tied specifically to the flaw; other times, the vulnerability is just an extra foible or phobia. In some films, it's a disability or a weakness. In *Hush*, a deaf woman is tormented. In *Jaws*, Brody is afraid of the water. Other times, it is more closely tied to the hero's arc, like in *The Exorcist*.

Hero: Father Damien Karras

Flaw: Struggling with his faith and feeling guilty for his mother's suffering.

Want: Initially wants to heal Regan, the possessed girl, through medical means.

Need: Ultimately needs to confront his loss of faith and self-doubt to perform the exorcism successfully.

Vulnerability: His faith and his guilt over choosing his vocation over his mom's needs. He's in a state of questioning—just the type of questioning a demon loves to exploit.

TRANSFORMATION & TRAGEDY

Your hero is going to start as a flawed individual and embark on a harrowing journey of change. Crafting the perfect course involves showing the hero's flaw and how it's messing with their lives. Then, through experiencing horror, they discover the need, ultimately removing their shard of glass, and forever fixing their flaw.

In the realm of horror, character journeys are best expressed as **before and afters.** The first step in crafting this chilling odyssey is to determine where your hero starts and where they will finish.

TRANSFORMATION: *The Descent*

BEFORE PICTURE: The hero, Sarah, begins as a grieving widow, haunted by the tragic loss of her husband and her daughter. She is consumed by survivor's guilt and withdrawn from her friends.

AFTER PICTURE: By the end of the film, Sarah transforms from a shattered and vulnerable woman into a fierce and determined survivor who faces off against the terrifying creatures lurking in the darkness.

TRANSFORMATION: *Midsommar*

BEFORE PICTURE: The hero, Dani, starts as a young woman grappling with profound grief and emotional instability after experiencing a devastating family tragedy.

AFTER PICTURE: By the film's conclusion, Dani undergoes a profound transformation, shedding her past traumas and embracing a newfound sense of belonging and agency.

TRANSFORMATION: *Get Out*

BEFORE PICTURE: The hero, Chris, begins as a young African-American man who is wary of visiting his white girlfriend's affluent family estate because of his experiences with racial microaggressions.

AFTER PICTURE: By the film's climax, Chris transforms from a passive victim into a resourceful and determined survivor who fights back against his oppressors.

DEFINING YOUR TRANSFORMATION MAP

A handy template to guide you through this character's journey is the **Transformation Map:**

Transformation Map = (DESCRIPTION OF FLAWED CHARACTER) learns (NEED or LESSON LEARNED) through (HIGH-LEVEL OVERVIEW OF SHOW'S STORY) and transforms to a (LESS FLAWED CHARACTER).

Transformation Map for *The Descent*:
(A grieving widow) learns (to embrace her inner strength) through (surviving an encounter with terrifying humanoid creatures in underground caves) and transforms into a (fierce and determined warrior no longer stunted by grief and guilts).

Transformation Map for *Midsommar*:
(A young woman grappling with profound grief and emotional instability) learns (empowerment and liberation) through (her mysterious and unsettling encounters with a Swedish commune's festival) and transforms into a (confident and liberated individual).

Transformation Map for *Get Out*:
(A young, insecure African-American man) learns (to confront racism head on) through (encountering the truth behind his white girlfriend's family's sinister plans) and transforms into a (bold, determined survivor).

THE HERO MUST TASTE BLOOD TO BE A MAN

The real test of a character arc is being able to answer "Yes" to the question: "Is the character we see at the end of the movie different than the one we saw at the start?"

Horror character arcs can be a little different. They're often less on the nose than other genres. Sometimes they don't have specific learning moments related to their needs and instead their ordeals are so harrowing and their minds are so tortured throughout the story, how can they *not* be transformed? They survive a trial by fire and, having been pushed to the primal edge of their sanity, we know they'll live differently. They've seen things no one is meant to see—they're wide-eyed to the evil that lurks in the world and now have a **survivor's perspective.**

The heroine of *The Descent* begins the movie as a grief-stricken person who can barely move on with life. However, after emerging from the harrowing encounter in the caves—where she saw her friend brutally killed but also discovered her inner warrior, which allowed her to escape and survive—we don't really ask, "I wonder if she'll still be overcome with the sorrow she had in the opening?" We can see the transformation. Her eyes are now wide open. She knows life is fickle. And she's proven by her warrior spirit—she wants to live!

Horror is often about a flawed hero being forced to tap into their deepest selves and realizing that they're a fierce survivor. That's a transformation that cures many flaws!

TRAGEDY & DOWN ENDINGS

Down endings are ones where the hero chooses not to learn the lesson presented by their needs... and things end badly. The audience can take away a positive in that they walk out of the theater high-fiving themselves, that they'd be smarter than the reckless movie heroes, and they'd adhere to the lesson. Life is fair.

On the other side of the coin, horror can be mean. Some movies present a nihilistic "bad things happen and there's nothing you can do about it" message. Often, these stories still depict a transformation, but despite all their personal growth, the heroes come to a horrific and shocking end. These finales undercut the hero's struggle and demonstrate a horrible unfair world—horror wins in the end.

You might be surprised that while down endings are common in the horror world, cynical/nihilistic ones are not. While there is an audience for the stark nihilism, it's rare for a horror story to have zero hope for humanity. These cynical stories tend to appear more in the Indy horror scene, where anything goes and attracting smaller niche audiences are "okay." Mostly, people don't want to be reminded how unfair the world is. They get those reminders in real life. That said, while horror is often escapist entertainment, even a happy ending usually carries a dark or cynical twist, reminding us that victory often has a price.

YOUR HERO'S ROOTING RESUME

One of the most common complaints fans have about horror stories is, "I didn't like any of the characters. I was rooting for them to die."

Outside of '80s Freddy Krueger and Jason Voorhees movies, stories that make audiences long for your characters to be killed off aren't good. Rooting interest in your heroes makes your movie more emotional, more fun and, most importantly... scarier. The first 10 percent of your story should go out of its way to get your audience on "Team Hero."

The goal is to make people worry about the fate of your heroes. If you do your job right, the audience will be so stressed about your hero's well-being, they'll keep their eyes open even when they know something horrible is about to happen. And that's when you get 'em... bwahahaha.

The whole idea of *Save the Cat!* is that if you give even the most despicable anti-hero a little moment where they do some act of kindness (like saving a kitty), we'll root for them.

That's good, and it still works, so if that's how you roll, go for it.

But I think it's just one part of a bigger strategy. I like to make a case for my heroes early in my stories. Even if they're horrible, they're complicated and have their good sides and opportunities to grow and learn.

This leads to the Rooting Resume. A **Rooting Resume** is a series of traits and moments that endear the hero to the audience. As you brainstorm your heroes, here are some of the most common traits of the Rooting Resume.

- THEY'RE UNDERDOGS – It's probably the best way to win our favor. We all feel like underdogs. We all have our reasons. We can relate to people that have an uphill climb. It gives us something to root for! This might mean they're alienated weirdos, societal outcasts, or misunderstood nerds akin to those we've seen wandering the eerie halls of high school horrors like *Carrie* or *Jennifer's Body*. The world may treat your heroes unjustly, like the main characters of *Don't Breathe* or the kids from *It*. Your heroes could be economically strapped, like the leads of *The Amityville Horror*. Or be boldly living their lives with a disease or a physical challenge like the deaf leads in *Hush* or *A Quiet Place*, or the wheelchair–bound boy in *Silver Bullet*. Or trying to play in the big leagues like the amateur filmmakers in *The Blair Witch Project*, or the out-of-their-league vampire experts like the Frog Brothers in *The Lost Boys* or Peter Vincent in *Fright Night*.

- THEY CARE ABOUT SOMEONE OR SOMETHING – It could be a kid, a significant other, a grandma, a friend, a crush, a family or even... here it comes... a cat! Think about the valiant parental protectors in *The Babadook* or *The Ring* or *A Quiet Place* or even Ripley protecting Newt in *Aliens*. Or the same cat lover Ripley in *Alien* or the family taking the cat in *Pet Semetary* or the heartfelt funeral for a pet bird in *Poltergeist*. Even caring for sweet, lovable Gizmo in *Gremlins* is endearing... just don't feed him after midnight. And though characters like the twisted lovers at the heart of *Hellraiser* are vile and unscrupulous, their motivations are clear and relatable, which helps us understand them—even if we don't agree with their murderous actions.

- THEY TRY VERY HARD TO MAKE THEIR LIVES BETTER – We love dreamers; they have lofty goals, a way out, or a plan. Even if they're failures, they tend to get up and try again. Think about Christine from *Drag Me to Hell*, who's willing to do what it takes to get that bank promotion. Then there's the leads from *Don't Breathe*, who are forced into a life of crime but long for a way out.
- THEY'RE FUN – If we like to be around the heroes, it goes a long way. Whether it's a gift of gab like Buffy the Vampire Slayer or the goofy one-liners of Ash from the *Evil Dead* series or the dry wit of Shaun from *Shaun of the Dead*, if characters are charming or sexy or sweet and adorkable, we'll root for them. Think of the lovable hillbillies from *Tucker & Dale*, or the charm and resourcefulness of Sidney from *Scream*.
- WE KNOW THEIR STRUGGLE – They have secret pain like the family in the Netflix series *The Haunting of Hill House*. They confess their flaws or we see them in personal moments. Often they're in mourning like the characters in *Hereditary* or *The Babadook* or *Midsommar*.
- WE WISH WE WERE MORE LIKE THEM – They're self-sacrificing, generous, resourceful, and loyal. Maybe they're the smartest person in the room. Maybe they're brave or resilient or just hugely capable leaders who take control of difficult situations. Examples include Ben in *Night of the Living Dead* or Rick in *The Walking Dead*, who take charge and assume difficult leadership positions for the good of the group.
- THEY'RE JUST LIKE US – Horror heroes often grapple with mundane woes, offering a mirror to our own existential dread, akin to the

fears of giving birth to a first child in *Rosemary's Baby* or the daily struggle of racism like *Get Out* or the shared grief of *Hereditary*.

- THEY'RE THE BEST AT SOMETHING – Heroes that are the best at something are always fascinating. Whether they're the best singer, the best butcher, the best driver... it's fun to "live" the lives of the most talented. Examples include Brian Cox in *The Autopsy of Jane Doe* or the Warrens in *The Conjuring* or the tortured best-selling novelist in *Misery*.

When working on your Rooting Resume, make sure your heroes tick more than one of these boxes. Most heroes tick several; some even all. There's no fixed number of Rooting Resume traits. You may even think of some outside of the above categories.

Later on, when you crank out scenes, you'll need to craft moments into the story that demonstrate the Rooting Resume in action. You'll need to create scenes in your story's Set-up beat—essentially the opening pages where we get to know your hero—that allow your audience to subconsciously check off Rooting Resume traits as they appear in your horror story.

THE FODDER... ERR... ENSEMBLE

Some writers have a hard time thinking up their ensemble. The way I like to think of them is they're "teachers of the need." They're there to show the character the way. Some are poor examples of how to live; some are good ones. Others are experts in the better way to live or represent the opposite point of view.

Your ensemble will teach your hero the lesson they need to learn. Decide how each character relates to the need:

- REJECTS THE NEED – A character that completely rejects the thing the hero needs to learn. Sometimes it's a villain or a nemesis. They share some similarities with the hero, but they fully reject the hero's core need with unwavering confidence—and, at least for now, it seems to be working out for them.

- NEEDS TO LEARN THE NEED – A person on a similar path to the hero. The hero might even see the flawed way of living in this person, because sometimes it's easier to see flaws in others.

- TAKES THE NEED TOO FAR – A person who goes so hard in the opposite direction that it turns into a flaw. Your hero is greedy and needs to learn to care for others more, but then this supporting character takes the need too far, being so generous that it borders on irresponsibility as they fail to provide for their own needs or those around them.
- TEACHES THE NEED – A mentor character that has it all figured out and can actively talk about what the hero needs to do better. These tend to be the Mr. Miyagis and Obi Wans of the world.
- LIVES THE NEED – People who are living examples of what the hero needs to learn and allow the hero to see the positive results of a different way of living and/or thinking.
- SUPPORTS THE NEED FOR CHANGE – The cheerleaders, the ones that want the best for the hero but maybe don't know exactly what that is or how to help them change.

Let's look at *Scream*'s ensemble cast and see how it uses these roles to teach Sidney Prescott's need:

Sidney Prescott (Main Character):
Needs to Learn the Need – As the main character, she needs to learn how to confront her past traumas to truly move forward with her life. Her mother was murdered a year ago. Sidney helped to put her killer away. But mom's backstory of being promiscuous and juggling many affairs has seemed to become the narrative, almost suggesting her mother deserved her tragic end. Sidney doesn't want to believe that and has shut down, refusing to confront the past and just sticking with her belief.

Ultimately, Sidney loses her virginity, survives, and uncovers the truth about her mother's past, realizing she was wrong about the killer. By confronting the past, she learns that life isn't like a horror movie—people are complex and can't be neatly categorized as simply "sinners" or not.

Gale Weathers:
Takes the Need Too Far – Gale is stuck in the past. She wants to rehash it, glorify it, and get new sales for her book. She's even right about the fact that the wrong man is behind bars for the murder, but she takes the need to such an extreme it only hurts the cause, instead of revealing the truth.

Dewey Riley:
Supports the Need for Change – While Dewey doesn't have any specific lessons to offer, he supports Sidney's need to heal. He often acts as a pillar of support for her throughout the series. He has a positive effect on Gale along the way, too.

Randy Meeks:
Rejects the Need – With his vast knowledge of horror movie tropes, Randy rejects the need because he feels the tropes resonate in real life and actually reinforce Sidney's greatest fear: that perhaps her mother deserved to die because of her promiscuous ways. This view of a binary good-vs.-evil world has forced Sidney to reject the nuance and complication that humans like her mother possess.

Billy Loomis:
Seems to Support the Need but Ultimately Takes the Need Too Far –At first, Billy represents as supportive. He seems more nuanced, understanding that Sidney's rigid view of the past isn't healthy, and realizing that perhaps things don't work like in the movies. Ultimately it's revealed he's the killer and his secret plan is to confront the past in the bloodiest way possible.

Stu Macher:
Rejects the Need – Stu goes along with Billy's plan for his own twisted reasons—in part to reenact a horror movie in real life—therefore believing in this binary "movie world" to its bloody and bitter end.

Tatum Riley:
Lives the Need – Tatum, Sidney's best friend, doesn't explicitly teach or reject the need, but she lives her life authentically and fearlessly, which indirectly influences Sidney to confront her fears.

Throughout the *Scream* series, each character in the ensemble plays a role in either supporting, rejecting, teaching, or embodying the lesson that Sidney needs to learn. Giving ensemble characters these thematic roles and perspectives allows you to play out the theme through the interactions of the main characters and their internal conflicts.

FINAL GIRLS & BOYS A.K.A. FINAL FOLK

The Texas Chainsaw Massacre popularized the notion that horror movies usually came down to one final survivor vs. the monster. This **Final Girl**

or Boy was most often the hero of the story—the one with the arc, need, theme, and transformation. This was the person Sam Raimi said needed to taste blood to become a man.

Back in the early days of horror, these final characters were a little thin on the development side. They tended to be one-dimensional characters whose sole purpose was to be tortured and tormented by the monster for maximum thrills.

Things have changed. There are plenty of stories that aren't just countdowns to the last sole survivor. Sometimes there are groups of people that survive together. There are even stories where no one dies. Also, we no longer just torment the women. The Final Girl trope has gone genderless. Let's call them **Final Folk.**

If you find yourself in a story that comes down to one of these Final Folk, make sure they have flaws and needs and be certain the horror transforms them. They'll come out the other side of their terrifying encounter having tasted blood—a rite of passage of sorts, where innocence is lost and a new type of warrior is born.

One big tip: make them fighters! Final Folk are scrappy, resilient, and ultimately need to fight back. And fight back hard. Even if they're underdogs, shy or scared, the horror unlocks something primal deep within them. When backed into a corner, they unleash an inner strength. They'll make smart decisions. Bold ones. Brave ones.

Most of their decisions won't work, so the Final Folk won't luck into survival, they'll earn every bloody drop of it. And the monster better watch out. Cause they just messed with the wrong person.

THE HALF-MAN

Monster in the House movies feature a unique mentor-type character who possesses knowledge and experience that can spell the difference between survival and annihilation. They're dubbed the **Half-Man** because they usually have survived encounters with the monster and have been left scarred in either physical and/or psychological ways.

The Half-Man often arrives in Act 2 when the monster is stirring trouble. Sometimes they show up as late as the Midpoint when the heroes seek help or information, like Tony Todd in *Final Destination*. Other times, they're embedded within the heroes but only emerge as the Half-Man later, like Ash in *Alien*. Some appear early but join the quest late in the game, like Quint in *Jaws*.

There are a few common Half-Man types:

1. THE SPIRITUAL GUIDE – A mystical or religious mentor who possesses supernatural knowledge and powers. Examples include Father Merrin (*The Exorcist*), Rham Jas (*Drag Me to Hell*), and Papa Justify (*The Serpent and the Rainbow*).

2. THE TRAGIC SURVIVOR – A character who has suffered at the hands of evil and has survived to warn others. Examples include Laurie Strode (*Halloween* series), Sidney Prescott (*Scream* series), Helen Lyle (*Candyman*).

3. THE PARANORMAL EXPERT/MONSTER HUNTER – A character who specializes in hunting and defeating supernatural creatures. Examples include Van Helsing (various Dracula adaptations), Abraham Setrakian (*The Strain* TV series), Dr. Woodman (*The Relic*).

4. THE FAKE EXPERT – Occasionally, the Half-Man you encounter is a fraud or somehow an expert in appearance only, but the knowledge—however dubious—helps the heroes battle the monster. Examples include Peter Vincent in *Fright Night* and the Frog Brothers in *The Lost Boys*.

5. DR. KNOWITALL – An expert who provides scientific explanations for the supernatural. Examples include Dr. Weir (*Event Horizon*) and Edwin Pollard (*Dark Skies*).

6. THE PSYCHIC – A character with psychic abilities who helps the heroes understand and combat the supernatural. Examples include Elise Rainier (*Insidious* series), Tangina Barrons (*Poltergeist*), Dick Holloran (*The Shining*).

7. THE LAW ENFORCEMENT OFFICER – A police officer or detective who helps investigate and fight against evil. Examples include Sheriff Brackett (*Halloween* sequels), Detective Muldoon (*The Grudge* - 2020), Sheriff John Hunt (*The Poughkeepsie Tapes*).

8. THE OCCULTIST – A person who practices magic or other esoteric arts. Examples include the fortune teller Rham Jas (*Drag Me to Hell*), suave occultist Duke de Richleau (from *The Devil Rides Out*), the collector of rare books in *The Ninth Gate*.
9. THE MONSTER STAN – A character who idolizes or serves the monster, like Igor (Frankenstein adaptations), Renfield (Dracula adaptations), or Ruth Harker in *Longlegs*, or even movie monster fans like Randy Meeks in *Scream*. Sometimes it could be a betrayer character who might be secretly allied with the monster, like Ash in *Alien*.
10. THE VENGEFUL SPIRIT – A supernatural force that's out to right a wrong but needs the help of the living to bring closure to their afterlives. Examples include the ghosts from *The Devil's Backbone* and *Lady in White*.

The Half-Man is a vital character in Monster in the House stories, offering essential knowledge or skills that may mean survival for the heroes. By drawing from their own terror-filled experiences with the monster, they act as both a warning and a guide, helping the heroes navigate the dangers ahead.

EXERCISES

1. Identify your hero's flaw, want, and need.
2. Define your hero's shard of glass, a pivotal moment or trauma from their past that serves as the origin of their flaws and vulnerabilities. This should be a defining event that shapes the character's journey and transformation.
3. Create a Transformation Map for your hero that outlines key stages of their character arc:
    1. Starting Point: Describe the hero's flaw and initial worldview.
    2. Catalyst: What event disrupts the hero's ordinary world and sets them on the path of change?
    3. Midpoint Crisis: Identify the moment of deep crisis or realization that challenges the hero's beliefs and compels them to confront their flaws.

4. Transformation: Describe the hero's final transformation, showing how they overcome their flaw and achieve personal growth.
5. Fill out the map: Transformation Map = (DESCRIPTION OF FLAWED CHARACTER) learns (NEED or LESSON LEARNED) through (HIGH-LEVEL OVERVIEW OF SHOW'S STORY) and transforms to a (LESS FLAWED CHARACTER).
6. Come up with a Rooting Resume for your hero. What are some of the reasons audiences will want to invite these people into their living room?
7. Ensemble Description: Describe how each ensemble character relates to the hero's theme and transformation arc. Assign roles based on their relationship dynamics:
    1. Rejecting the Need – Characters who challenge or oppose the hero's growth.
    2. Needing to Learn the Need – Characters who mirror the hero's initial flaws or lack awareness.
    3. Taking the Need Too Far – Characters who embody an extreme version of the hero's flaw or desire.
    4. Teaching the Need – Mentors or guides who impart wisdom and guidance to the hero.
    5. Living the Need – Characters who already embody the hero's desired state, serving as inspiration.
    6. Supporting the Need for Change – Allies or supporters who assist the hero in their transformation journey.
8. Imagine the monster never showed up in your story. In a few sentences, describe the compelling drama that would play out.

PART 4:
LAYING DOWN THE BONES: CRAFTING THE HORROR NARRATIVE

CHAPTER 10: HORROR STORY STRUCTURE

The idea of writing a 300-page novel or a 100-page screenplay or even a 60-page TV pilot is daunting. But if you can break it into chunks—smaller, more manageable tasks—maybe, just maybe, it's less impossible. Lucky for us, the original master of horror, creepy old Aristotle himself, broke stories into 3 parts. It's a little something he called 3-Act Spooky Structure. It generally goes like this:

A **Beginning** where characters are introduced and conflict is turned on.
A **Middle** where characters deal with conflict.
An **End** where the conflict is resolved in a satisfying and cathartic way.
Or... paraphrasing...

ACT 1: Get your heroes trapped in a cabin with a monster.
ACT 2: Have the monster attack the cabin.
ACT 3: Get the heroes out of the cabin and back to safety.

Note, the second act is the most fun. It's the monster! The scares! The kills! The terror! It's the whole reason we love horror. For this reason, the second act is given double the time, i.e., Act 2 is as long as Acts 1 and 3 combined. In a 100-minute movie, it might breakdown into something like:

Act 1 = 25 minutes
Act 2 = 50 minutes
Act 3 = 25 minutes

So now we've turned one impossible task into three slightly less impossible ones.

But it's still a lot.

And even watching someone get chased by masked chainsaw-wielding maniacs gets old after 50 minutes. A good Act 2 needs twists and turns and moments that ramp up tension and make life harder and harder for the good guys.

One way to ensure a big twist is to split Act 2 down the middle—with a Midpoint—giving us a logical "gearshift" moment in the story. A moment that raises the stakes (and therefore "dimes" the tension on the old tension meter).

Splitting Act 2 in half morphs our old-school 3-act structure into 4 Acts.

Four manageable parts.

Cool, right?

But still hard.

In the words of Dr. Frankenstein, "We need more parts!"

What if we could break your horror story into 15 manageable parts?

That would be even easier, right?

Good news, somebody already did it.

BLAKE SNYDER'S *SAVE THE CAT!* BEAT SHEET

The *Save the Cat!* "beat sheet" is a tool that breaks down a story into 15 main parts, or "beats." Each beat represents an essential moment in the story's structure, moving the plot forward in meaningful ways.

So, what exactly is a beat?

A **beat** is simply a storytelling moment. It could be a single moment within a scene or a larger sequence of events. Think of it as the smallest building block of the story's structure. Here's an example from *Halloween*:

- Dr. Loomis arrives at the mental hospital and sees that patients are wandering around outside, signaling that something is very wrong.
- Michael Myers then steals Loomis's car and escapes.

These two moments are each beats—they're key moments that move the story forward, creating a sequence of "And then, and then, and then..." that builds suspense and tension.

Beats can also be bigger sequences or groups of scenes that move the story along in a significant way. Take this example from *The Conjuring*:

- The Warrens, paranormal investigators, enter the haunted house and begin investigating. They discover an eerie, dark force lurking in the basement.

Here, the entire investigation can be considered a beat, even if it contains multiple scenes.

When outlining, you're aiming to capture these big-picture story moves without getting bogged down in every small detail. A **beat sheet** is essentially Step 1: it's the structural blueprint of the story before you dive into writing out each scene in detail.

Think about how you'd summarize your favorite horror movie in five minutes. You might start with a sequence like:

• A girl swims in the ocean at night and is suddenly attacked by a shark. Blood in the water.

Then go to the next key moment:

• We meet Brody, a sheriff in a small beach town. He's got a wife and kids, and he's just learned there was a shark attack.

And then...

• Brody goes out to the beach and finds the girl's remains.

Each of these "And then..." moments is a beat—a point that moves the story forward and keeps building suspense.

You could outline an entire story like this. Many writers do. They just start jotting down scenes and story beats on a series of notecards and organizing them until the story emerges and solidifies.

But it's easier and more effective if you have some guidance. Some plan. Some way to know what you're missing and when you're done.

The *Save the Cat!* beat sheet is a series of 15 beats every good story must have. It's a way to plan out your story and ensure you're not missing anything important.

Here's a quick description of the 15 beats. (Since we're talking general story here, we'll use percentage markers instead of page counts or minute designations in the parentheses below.):

THE *SAVE THE CAT!* BEAT SHEET

ACT 1: The Ordinary World – Thesis

1. OPENING IMAGE (0-1%) – A thematic or grabbing visual image, scene, or brief sequence which sets the tone of your movie. It often serves as the "before" picture of your hero (or world) who will transform throughout the story.

2. THEME STATED (5%) – A line of dialogue that organically states what your story is all about. The theme is typically voiced by another character to your hero, calling out the hero's deeper flaw or spiritual need for genuine change.

3. SET-UP (1%-10%) – Reveals your main character's "ordinary life" or status quo. Takes time to lay down a character's flaws and how those flaws caused

a life that really needs to be shaken up. Describes the character's world for home, work, and play, and introduces the important secondary characters who play a part in the hero's life.

4. CATALYST (10%) – The life-changing moment that happens to the hero and sets the story in motion. Provides that initial shove onto the story rollercoaster.

5. DEBATE (10%-20%) – The reaction to the Catalyst, usually presented as a question ("Do I really have to go on this dangerous quest?"). Can be a sequence of doubt, denial, evasion, or even preparation. It lends weight to the life-changing bigger journey yet to come, prepping the new world as one that you do not enter lightly.

ACT 2: The Upside-Down World – Antithesis

6. BREAK INTO 2 (20%) – The hero takes action and locks in to accomplish a goal, venturing into a new world, or choosing a new way of thinking. This is a decisive action that separates the old/ordinary world from the new world.

7. B STORY (22%) – A thematic secondary story is kicked off. Often, this is a story about love or friendship or mentorship.

8. FUN & GAMES (20%-50%) – The hero in the new world. This beat delivers on the *promise of the premise*. It's a large section of the story that essentially shows "the movie you came to see." Contains scenes and sequences that are shown in the trailer of movies or hinted at in the blurb on the back of the book or on that "Coming Next Week" teaser at the end of a TV show.

9. MIDPOINT (50%) – The middle of the story and culmination of the Fun & Games. Usually, this beat is a *false victory* or a *false defeat*. The Midpoint *raises the stakes* for the hero, forcing them to narrow their focus on winning the day or surviving. Often, a *ticking clock* is introduced here, furthering tension and upping the urgency.

10. BAD GUYS CLOSE IN (50%-75%) – Stakes have raised and tension is higher. Bad Guys may be literally closing in or psychological/internal Bad Guys may cause more problems.

11. ALL IS LOST (75%) – The moment the hero most feared actually happens. Now it looks like the hero will lose. Usually contains a *whiff of death* where someone has died or the threat of actual death is in the air. This is the hero's rock-bottom moment.

12. DARK NIGHT OF THE SOUL (75%-80%) – A reaction to the All Is Lost where a hero wallows in sadness, mourning what was lost and lamenting that they are now worse off than before the story began. This is an opportunity to take stock, where meaningful learning happens on the way to transformation.

ACT 3: Merged World – Synthesis

13. BREAK INTO 3 (80%) – A new piece of information is discovered, and the hero realizes what they must do to solve all the problems that have been created in Act 2.

14. FINALE (80%-99%) – The big showdown where the hero finally proves they've learned the lesson that was taught via their struggles in Act 2. The quest is won, the dragon is slain, and when the smoke clears the hero has changed. Their flaw is repaired, and the world is indeed a better place.

15. FINAL IMAGE (99%-100%) – The "after photo" of the hero and the world. This mirror image of the Opening Image shows how far the world and the hero have transformed.

Okay, let's look at a quick example. Since Blake already "beat out" a Monster in the House movie, *Alien*, in one of his books, let's do *Aliens*. Writer/director James Cameron is great at story structure.

As a kid, I saw *Aliens* in a packed Friday night theater. It was the single most intense viewing experience of my life. It had everything... laughs, action, dread, tension, and SCARES. I think I dug a hole in my armrests. It's still one of my favorite movies and one of the most structurally solid screenplays ever.

***Aliens* Beat Sheet**

Opening Image: We open where we left Ripley at the end of the first movie in the *Alien* series. She sleeps inside a spaceship's cryofreeze bed. She's the lone survivor of the first movie (well, her and the cat... which she saved). A salvage ship finds her and rescues her.

Set-Up: Recovering in a medical bed, she discovers she was out there in space for 57 years and is haunted by the horrors she experienced, having nightmares about the alien bursting out of her gut. The company seems to blame the whole encounter on Ripley. They don't believe her story about the alien and her bloody battle for survival. She discovers that the planet where they found the alien now has a colony of inhabitants that are terraforming it.

Theme Stated: In the theatrical version, Ripley's arc is about overcoming the horror of the first movie. It's sort of a "take control of your fear by facing it again" arc. But in the originally planned version seen in the extended edition, Ripley finds out her daughter is dead. She missed out on her whole life. She had promised she'd be home for her 11th birthday. This is the ghost that's haunting her. It tracks strong as an arc when she becomes a protector of a little girl who is the lone survivor of the colony.

Catalyst: Burke visits Ripley to inform her that they lost contact with the colony on the planet and want her to join the rescue mission.

Debate: She's not interested. Burke makes a case: they'd be going with space marines. They want her as an advisor. She still refuses. She's not going back.

Break into 2: She wakes up from a night terror and looks in the mirror. She won't get over this unless she faces her fear. She asks Burke if he's going to destroy the monster. He assures her that is their intent. She's in.

B Story: The B Story kicks off a little later here (this is a floating beat that moves around a little), but the "love story" at the heart of *Aliens* is Ripley and Newt. Ripley becomes the mother figure for Newt, battling against the villainous mother figure the Alien Queen. It begins about halfway through the Fun & Games when they discover Newt hiding in the complex. But first, we have to get to the planet.

Fun & Games: The spaceship and crew travel to the derelict colony. Ripley meets the team, a bunch of arrogant space marines and an android named Bishop, who she's suspicious of after her bad encounter with Ash, an android in the first movie who betrayed her and her crew. They reach the planet and go out to explore. Once there, they find no colonists, only wreckage and signs of a brutal struggle and evidence of the aliens (damage from acid blood, face-hugger specimens). And here's where the B Story kicks in. They find one survivor: a little girl named Newt. Thematically in tune with the extended edition, Ripley becomes her surrogate protector throughout the remainder of the film.

The team realizes the colony has been turned into breeding hosts for the monsters. As they venture deeper into the lair, there are more and more troubling signs and ultimately the aliens attack! This time there's more than one creature... it's *Aliens*! And they attack!

Midpoint: Ripley and company fight their way to safety and decide to nuke the entire colony from space to destroy the beasts, but it's a *false victory*. When they call for transport, it crashes (an alien having snuck its way onboard). Now they're stranded and night is coming. And the aliens mostly come at night...

Bad Guys Close In: The gang seals off certain hallways to create a barricade. But they realize the transport's crash has set into motion a potential explosion that will occur in four hours (*ticking clock*). They come up with a plan for Bishop to go out and use the colony's communication to remote control a new transport from their orbiting ship, while they try to fight off the monsters to stay alive. The monsters come and the battle is hellish, taking out everyone except Hicks (who is injured), Ripley, and Newt.

All Is Lost: Newt is captured by an alien and taken back to their nest, deep in the bowels of the colony.

Dark Night of the Soul: Hicks is gravely injured, and Ripley's now effectively on her own. Bishop's return with the rescue ship offers a chance to escape, but Ripley knows she can't leave without Newt, even if it means facing almost certain death.

Break into 3: Ripley gears up and pilots the ship deep into the alien's kill zone. She's going on a rescue mission.

Finale: With the complex on the verge of exploding, Ripley enters the monster's lair and faces off with horrors (most notably the Alien Queen) as she rescues Newt. Bishop is there to haul them away as the whole place explodes. Newt and Ripley have a touching moment onboard. But there's one more battle to be fought: the Queen has snuck aboard and ripped apart Bishop. Ripley battles the creature with the mechanical loader and ultimately slays the beast by vanquishing it out into space.

Final Image: Ripley and Newt go into cryofreeze and we see them sleeping peacefully for the long ride home.

The ins and outs of beat sheets can fill an entire book... or several! But here's more good news—those books have already been written. If you're new to *Save the Cat!* or want a more granular, deep dive into each of the beats, I recommend you visit *savethecat.com* and either check out their many free resources or pick up one of the earlier books in the series. They're great and there's a ton to learn about structure and how to use those beats for all their worth.

But for now, let's dive into how these beats apply specifically to horror stories.

CHAPTER 11: SLOW BURN vs. RELENTLESS HORROR

Horror stories typically fall into two main structural types: **relentless horror** and **slow burn**. Each type shares horror fundamentals, but the way tension and suspense are delivered differs significantly.

RELENTLESS HORROR

While prepping *The Evil Dead*, Andy Grainger, a friend of actor Bruce Campbell and writer/director Sam Raimi, gave them one piece of advice: "Fellas, no matter what you do, keep the blood running down the screen."

I've always taken this to heart. Once you flip the switch and unleash the beast in your story, keep the blood running down the screen.

In **relentless horror**, the monster is unleashed at the Break into 2 and it's game on! The Story DNA of relentless horror promises a primal story where the hero's goal is survival, the obstacle is the monster, and the stakes are literally life and death. These stories are fast-paced, urgent, and... relentless. They pin their foot on the gas pedal and don't let up until the end.

Here are some examples:

In *Scream*, Act 1 introduces a group of high school students who are targeted by a masked killer known as Ghostface. The goal for the protagonists is to survive and evade Ghostface's relentless pursuit. The main obstacle is the unpredictable and unrelenting killer. Will they survive? Or will they die?

In *Train to Busan*, Act 1 introduces a diverse group of passengers on a speeding train bound for Busan, South Korea. As the journey unfolds, they find themselves amid a sudden and catastrophic zombie outbreak. The goal for the protagonists is to survive the relentless onslaught of the undead and reach the safety of Busan, where they believe they will find refuge from the horrors outside.

In *The Purge*, Act 1 sets up a near-future America where all crime is legalized for one night every year. The goal for the protagonists is to survive the night of the Purge and protect their family from the dangerous forces gathering outside their door.

In *A Quiet Place: Day One*, the first act introduces a terminally ill cancer patient reluctantly participating in a group outing to Manhattan. As the group enjoys a marionette show, chaos erupts when deadly, sound-sensitive creatures begin to wreak havoc across the city. The goal for the protagonists is simple but primal: survive the sudden and violent onslaught of these alien predators.

In each of these relentless horror films, the goal (to survive) and the main obstacle (the monsters) are established by the end of Act 1, setting the stage for a gripping and tension-filled narrative as the characters fight to live through the nightmarish ordeals they face.

Relentless horror functions like most other good stories. The stakes are huge, the goal is simple and primal, and watching the hero navigate impossible obstacles and unrelenting evil is the fun.

SLOW BURN HORROR

By contrast, **slow burn horror** doesn't unleash the full threat early on, creating suspense by gradually building unease and mystery. Rather than entering a straightforward survival mode at the Break into Two, the hero often grapples with strange or subtle threats that only later reveal their true, often horrifying nature. In these films, the Fun & Games section teases the terror, introducing our heroes to an upside-down world filled with mystery, uncertainty, and dread.

Slow burners are not as clear cut. They can be difficult to pull off. A frequent problem I find in the work of new writers is that they accidentally stumble into stories that are slow burns. They'll send me a screenplay about a vampire and I'll get to page 30 and there's no sign of bloodsuckers. Page 50, still no undead or goals or obstacles. Page 60 or 70, the vampire finally shows up and then I only get 10-20 pages of blood-sucking fun in a 100-page script. That's barely a vampire script at all.

To compound this issue, if you're reading a story cold (i.e., you haven't read its logline or heard its pitch or watched its trailer), these scripts can be wildly frustrating because you're constantly asking, "What's this about?" or

"What's the story?" or even "What genre is this?" You keep waiting for the plot to kick in. And waiting. And waiting...

These unintentional slow burns are often written by new writers who are learning the ins and outs of story structure.

Still, there are many great horror stories that don't kick off a full-on survival story at the Break into 2. These slow burns happen more in horror than in any other genre.

Why?

Well, tension is the fuel to story and **dread** is the *tension du jour* of horror. Slow burn horror pours on the dread like an elevator at the Overlook Hotel pours on the blood. Even though the monster might not be relentlessly attacking the hero throughout the early part of these stories, we're constantly reminded and warned that the beast is coming. There's no escape. The worry and the fear of the inevitable evil swells within us minute by minute, second by second. There's no time to be bored. We're too busy digging our fingernails into the armrests of our chairs.

You'll know you're in a slow burn situation if you struggle with a logline. Slow burns typically have elevator pitches that need to cheat a little. They include goals, obstacles, and stakes that lock in later than the Break into 2 (in slow burns they often wait until the Midpoint), or you're scrambling to add other stuff outside of your Story DNA to make it seem more active and less vague and have a bit more sizzle. In slow burn stories, it can be a struggle to define your hero's goal because they don't have one that's very "premise worthy" until some big Act 2 revelation.

Let's look at these quick pitches for some slow burn movies:

Get Out – After a young African-American man visits his white girlfriend's family for the weekend, he must uncover the sinister truth behind their seemingly benevolent facade to escape with his life or else become a victim of a twisted conspiracy to transplant his consciousness into another body.

The main character, while on edge and tense about meeting his white girlfriend's family, doesn't really suspect the wild life-or-death stuff until halfway through the movie. But that makes for a boring logline. The setting and situation is filled with weirdness and dread and tension... like the weird hypnosis scene and the African-American help acting almost zombie-like... but there's no real goal for the hero (not even solving the mystery of what's going on is that critical to the hero) until around the Midpoint when he sees someone from the past who went missing. Only then does the hero's titular goal of "GETTING OUT" kick in.

This happens in a lot of slow burn horror movies. The monster operates behind the scenes. The slow burn story is filled with dread and mystery and a basic winding tension that you know is just going to snap, eventually.

Creepy haunted house movies like *Paranormal Activity* or *The Conjuring* or even movies like *Alien* tease the terror until around the Midpoint when it's fully unleashed. Even many slashers have the monster killing people in the shadows and lurking... but the monster doesn't go "Game on!" until about halfway through.

Jurassic Park – After a billionaire entrepreneur creates a theme park populated with genetically engineered dinosaurs, a group of survivors must navigate the island overrun by escaped predators to reach safety or else face being hunted down and eaten by creatures long extinct.

Sounds like a lot of dinosaurs eating people in the Fun & Games, right? Well, no. The monsters-run-amok stuff doesn't kick in until about halfway into the movie (around the 60-minute mark) when the park's power goes out during a botched heist and all the safeguards come down. *Jurassic Park* really has a double premise: "Imagine a theme park with cloned dinosaurs" and "What if people were trapped in a theme park with cloned dinosaurs?"

Spielberg likes doing a thing where his stories start with awe and wonder then go dark. *Gremlins*, *Close Encounters of the Third Kind*, and *Poltergeist* are other examples. Like those stories, *Jurassic Park* takes the time to milk the wish-fulfillment. It still has to find tension with hints that the danger is to come and chaos theory will prevail and we'll be seeing lots of T-Rex and Raptor vs. human action soon enough.

The Exorcist – After a young girl becomes possessed by a malevolent entity, a determined priest must perform an exorcism to save her soul and banish the demon from her body or else witness the corruption and the destruction of innocence at the hands of unspeakable evil.

In this logline, it feels like it's all priest vs. demon. But in the film, the priest isn't even called in until around the THIRD act! This would be like the logline from *Star Wars: A New Hope* pitching the Death Star attack sequence as the primary premise of that story. Instead, *The Exorcist*'s slow burn plot spends most of the time in investigative territory, a sort of "What's going on with my daughter?" as the supernatural malady grows worse and worse and worse.

There are lots of other classic horror movies that are slow burns. In *Halloween*, Laurie Strode doesn't know she's definitely in trouble until close to the 75 percent mark of the movie. In a movie like *M3GAN* or other domestic thrillers, the audience knows there's a monster in the house, but the monster doesn't become truly confrontational until around the Midpoint or later.

Slow burn doesn't necessarily mean slow-paced either. *Aliens* is essentially a slow burn film. It mirrors the beats of the atmospheric, deliberately paced original *Alien*. The monster doesn't show until the Midpoint when the battle for survival kicks off. But I dare anyone to say *Aliens* is ever boring. It rips off a ton of story—Ripley's backstory, the missing colony, the introduction of marines, the exploration of the colony and the mysteries wherein—at a fast pace... it's just not the relentless battle for survival we get at the Midpoint.

MAKING SLOW BURN HORROR WORK

Conflict hooks the audience. The primary source of tension in a script is a hero with a goal encountering an obstacle. If you hold off on establishing this fundamental source of conflict in your stories, other methods of deriving tension need to go on overdrive (mystery, dread, internal struggles) or substitute "goals" need to be temporarily put into place until the real life-or-death plot stuff kicks in. Aimless heroes who are waiting around for something to happen are often the death of story. Lack of character agency can lead to episodic and random storytelling. It can be boring.

Imagine the monster is a disease. Relentless horror delivers a sudden heart attack that the patient must battle through urgently to survive. The story focuses on the hero's desperate attempt to stem off death.

Slow burn horror is like a disease that gradually takes hold. Symptoms present themselves, but the hero might just carry on with life without paying it much thought. Eventually questions are raised. Heroes may investigate the root cause, ignore it, or even try to fix it in wrong ways. Information might be sought out. Friends and family may try to gaslight the hero. All the while, the disease intensifies... until it becomes the sole undeniable focus of the hero's attention.

Slow burn works best when the elements of the monster infiltrating the ordinary world are filled with tension and fun in ways that may be more resonant and impactful than a direct attack. Like in *Paranormal Activity*, witnessing the supernatural forces slowly seep into the hero's very familiar and realistic ordinary world is intriguing and allows us to imagine the "what if this happened to us" of it all. The parts at the end where the demon possesses our hero are well done and important to the overall narrative, but the film's slow realistic tease is the highlight of such a story.

These narratives play with their food, making audiences think the monster can strike at any time as they inch the hero more and more into dangerous territory. Tension simmers like a pot on a low flame, gradually intensifying the fear and the apprehension until it reaches a boiling point. In these stories, the audience is often more in the know than the hero and thus tends to be more stressed than the hero. The hero's lack of urgency only adds to the story's tension, as we hope they'll figure it out before it's too late.

Here are four techniques (of many) that slow burn stories use to keep the audience's attention before the big inevitable battle for survival that will come in the second half of the story:

TECHNIQUE 1: FUN & GAMES... & MORE DEBATE!

The Fun & Games section usually functions as a Fun & Games... & More Debate section. The heroes grapple with uncertainty and the ambiguity of the threat they face. The Break into 2 marks a definitive shift in the story, but questions and doubts still linger. There are still some questions about the monster in the air: "What is the cause of these symptoms?" "Is the monster real?" "Can I ignore it and let it go away?"

To delineate from the first act, the Break into 2 often answers some specific question that leads to new ones. Like the beat might communicate, "Yes, my house is haunted... but can I live with it?" or "Sure, I have a monster but are they good or evil?" or "Yes, my daughter is acting weird... but can medical science fix the problem?" The hero might try to carry on with their regular lives while juggling the pursuit of answers to the lingering monster questions.

Here's another way to look at it: Some slow burn stories have long first acts—first acts that take up half the movie. And while you could look at it that way, I prefer the Fun & Games & Debate approach, as it's more instructive in my outlines and you're more likely to keep the long "Debate" interesting. If you have a 60-minute Act 1, then all the other beats like Fun & Games, Midpoint, and Bad Guys Close In seem squeezed or rushed. There's a tendency to force them in inorganically.

If you find yourself in this Long Act 1 scenario, consider the Fun & Games... & More Debate model.

TECHNIQUE 2: SCARES IN THE SHADOWS

One way to make slow burn horror work is to show the audience that the monster is operating in the shadows, outside of the direct attention of your hero. Much like the Opening Scare, it gives the audience a "superior position," promising an inevitable confrontation with the monster.

Some movies deliver a Scare in the Shadows every 10 minutes or so. It keeps stories "on schedule" with their scares-per-minute while allowing a slow burn plot to simmer. Each scare (or often kill in a slasher film) feels one step closer to the collision the monster will have with the hero. It gives the audience the thrills and the chills they expect while allowing the benefits of a slow burn structure to play out. You see this a lot in slashers like *Halloween*, where Michael Myers is adding to his kill count and the movie's scare beats while Laurie Strode is mostly unaware of the killing spree until late in the movie.

TECHNIQUE 3: DRAMA, DRAMA, DRAMA

Besides amping up the dread, a lot of slow burn horror focuses on that "drama story" that Jason Blum talked about. The dramatic "non-monster" story needs to be compelling enough that audiences will forgive the wait for the monster-ey goodness.

In these stories, the hero's goal in Act 1 will often be about a troubled relationship, a stressful job, a difficult move, the loss of a family member, the fracturing of a relationship, or some other dramatic conflict in their life. Within these "real world" problems, the malevolent force finds its foothold, subtly interfering and entangling itself in the characters' lives. As the sinister elements unfold, the monster is slowly revealed to be an external threat intertwined with the protagonists' inner struggles and conflicts.

For example, *Hereditary* tracks a family dealing with grief while the monster lurks in the background. *M3GAN* follows a young woman accepting the responsibilities of raising her late sister's daughter while still maintaining her high-tech career. *Get Out* is about a young African American man navigating his white girlfriend's world.

TECHNIQUE 4: FUN & GAMES IS DREAD & GAMES!

Lay on the dread. Later, in Chapter 13, I'll describe many techniques to add dread to your story. Dread, or the anticipation of some horrible thing that's about to happen, works best when it's not interrupted by tons of scares. In slow burn stories, dread is the star. Dread, dread, and more dread will keep the audience squirming in their seats. They'll be too stressed to say, "When's the monster going to show up?" Dread is the special sauce that separates the great slow burn stories from the "slow-paced" ones.

In Chapter 14, I'll break down both a slow burn horror and a relentless horror so we can compare the differences in action. But first (after the exercises below) we'll look at some other things that horror beat sheets do differently.

EXERCISES

1. We still have a few more important things to discuss before it's time to start filling out beat sheets. For now, determine if you're writing a relentless or slow burn horror story. Are you telling a story where the Fun & Games is a life-or-death battle of man vs. monster? Or is it a slow burn story where the monster is lurking in the shadows, messing with people's minds and lives? Is the Fun & Games more about tension and mystery and less about survival?
2. If your story is slow burn, at what beat do you plan to fully unleash your monster? Somewhere in Fun & Games? The Midpoint? Later?
3. If you're writing a slow burn, list some ways your story can keep audience attention with tension, mystery, and the dramatic story.
4. It's probably a good time to revisit your Story DNA and logline, especially if you're creating a slow burn horror story. Firm that up in preparation for filling out your beat sheet.

CHAPTER 12: THE MAD SCIENCE OF HORROR BEAT SHEETS

The beat sheet has been used effectively by horror writers since Blake introduced it many years ago. I've been using it to write my scary stories for almost 20 years. And throughout those years, I've noticed some deviations or common threads specific to the horror genre. This chapter looks at some Frankenstein-ing you can do with your beat sheets to give you some further guidance and inspiration. Let's dive in.

OPENING IMAGE EQUALS OPENING SCARE

Kicking horror movies off with a scare has been around since *Halloween*, *Night of the Living Dead*, and *The Exorcist*. But in the world of streaming, it's practically mandatory. Grabbing attention within the first three minutes has proven to be super-critical in all genres. People will give movies, shows, and books a quick try but move on to some other content if you don't deliver the goods ASAP. Even beyond producers and studios who demand "one scare beat every 10 minutes," putting a scare beat up front buys you 10-12 minutes of ordinary world and character set-up that doesn't have to deliver a big scare or even a heavy dose of dread.

An **opening scare** allows the writer to establish tone and genre right from the get-go. It buys the narrative some much needed time by planting the seed of what's coming and setting your audience at ease that the story ahead is indeed a horror story. It's a contract of sorts: "Hey, it's okay, this is a horror story. We'll get to the scary stuff. Promise."

There are a few common types of opening scares:

- FIRST KILL – The most common way to open a horror story is to show the monster's first kill. A classic example is the initial shark attack in *Jaws* or the Drew Barrymore scene in *Scream*. This first kill is often a mini-story that could work as a short film unto itself. (In fact, several horror films have been born out of first-kill-style proof of concept short films that went on to be adapted into features.) Sometimes this is the "last kill before the monster is noticed" in that the horror is ongoing in the world, but this is the one bloody incident that immediately proceeds the events of the movie before your heroes become entangled in it all.

- FLASH-FORWARD – Other stories jump ahead to show something that will happen in the middle or toward the end of the film. These scenes give a taste of the urgency, danger, and tension to come. The narrative then flashes back to the story's true beginning and reveals the events leading up to that moment. These glimpses of the future plant a major question in the audience's brains: "How did things get so bad?" This knowledge of what lays ahead for your heroes puts your audience in a superior position (i.e., they know more than the characters) and winds up the tension since they know what danger lies ahead.

  Rise of the Evil Dead uses this technique. It shows a horrific supernatural attack, then flashes back to one day earlier, introducing our real main characters and leaving us to ask: Who are those people we just saw and how do they ultimately collide with this horror story that begins to unfold?

  Another Ghosthouse picture, *Don't Breathe*, uses a flash-forward too.

  In my opinion, the flash-forward is a bit of a cheat and not always as satisfying as the other methods. A lot of times when I see a flash-forward with aspiring screenwriters, it's sort of a crass attempt to open with horror. Yet it can be effective when the other methods don't work.

- THE ORIGIN OF THE HORROR – *Halloween* opens with a child—who will become our killer—committing his first murder before being sent away to an institution for several years. In *Hellraiser*, the opening shows a person messing with the puzzle box that brings about the demons and their horrific effects. While this moment isn't the origin of the puzzle box, it lays the backstory for the individual who is the true villain of the piece fighting to get his flesh back. *28 Days Later* opens with animal rights activists breaking into a research facility where chimpanzees are being experimented on with a virus called "Rage." When one activist is attacked by an infected chimp, the virus spreads rapidly, leading to a catastrophic outbreak of zombie-like creatures.

- THE HORROR BEFORE THE HORROR – Some stories begin with a horrific moment that has nothing to do with the monster. A sudden shock or scare or gross-out moment often reveals the hero's backstory (their shard of glass), injecting grief or guilt or anger as a thematic weight on the main characters. For example, the opening of *Midsommar* depicts the terrifying suicide of the main character's sister. Both *The Descent* and *M3GAN* open with tragic accidents that establish the emotional baggage of the main characters. In these films, a horrific moment often haunts the main character and informs their flaws and needs.
- THE DREAD START – In some stories, the monster and scares are saved for later, when they crash into the hero's life. These can still start with moments of tension, setting the stage for dread and foreshadowing the horrors to come. Think of the dark, almost lifeless spaceship at the start of *Alien*, where the crew of space truckers lie death-like in cryo-freeze coffins. Similarly, *Hereditary* opens with the slow burn of familial grief, creating an atmosphere so oppressive that the audience senses the impending terror, even though the actual horror hasn't yet begun. These openings give a quiet but unnerving sense that something isn't right, ramping up the suspense until the true nightmare unfolds.

There are exceptions to starting with a scare or even using your opening to slowly drip-feed tension and dread. This happens mostly in stories where you want the audience to experience the surprise and shock of the horrific elements as the hero does.

Movies like *A Quiet Place: Day One*, *Barbarian*, *The Blair Witch Project*, and *The Texas Chainsaw Massacre* set up a sense of normalcy or complacency that creates a different kind of tension—the tension of knowing the horror is coming, but the question is... *when*?

Strategically, for writers trying to sell first novels or stories, or for streamers trying to grab attention-deprived audiences, kicking off with a scene that delivers a jolt of "horror goodness" and promises more scares along the way just makes sense. Choose the right opening for your story carefully.

THE CATALYST IS ABOUT THE HERO, NOT THE MONSTER

Many writers get the "Opening Horror" confused with the Catalyst. The Catalyst beat happens to the hero. For example, the opening death scene in *Jaws* feels like a catalyst, but imagine if that body was never found or the Coast Guard took over. Those wouldn't be incidents that moved Chief Brody from the ordinary world to the story world. Therefore, the Catalyst in *Jaws* is when he finds the half-eaten body on the beach. It's the first moment that suggests he'll be leaving his ordinary world and stepping into the upside-down world of a horror story.

Double-check your Catalyst. Make sure it is specifically about something happening *to* your hero.

THE 'WE'RE TRAPPED WITH A MONSTER!' BEAT

This is a floating beat that can happen anywhere between the Catalyst and the Break into 3. It's the moment the hero realizes they're trapped with the monster and in a battle for survival. In relentless horror, this will commonly be the Break into 2. In slow burn, it will be later... sometimes at the Midpoint and sometimes at the All Is Lost. The engine of slow burn tends not to be a battle for survival.... to the characters... but as the audience, we know the battle is coming—we're ahead of the heroes. While they're fussing around with other things or distractions, we know the final battle is inevitable.

THE 'IN THE HANDS OF A MADMAN' MOMENT

Blake Snyder insisted on the *Save the Cat!* moment. For horror, I'm going to insist on the **In the Hands of a Madman** moment. I guess I should've called it *Skin the Cat!* or something on brand. But I love cats, so we'll go with the Madman thing.

If you can convince the audience that ANYTHING can happen early in a story, it jacks up the tension to a maximum. Sometimes the best way to do this is to turn a trope on its head. Push the boundaries of what is safe in a story to the edge. Do something taboo or slightly beyond the bounds of taste. Or use audience expectations against them to up the horror. Whatever gives the audience hope or safety or relief... crush it and crush it hard in a way that you say, "This isn't other movies! YOU ARE NOT SAFE!!"

This In the Hands of a Madman moment is usually found at or before the Midpoint. The earlier, the better. Because once you do it, it unsettles the audience. And if you can do that, even the most mundane scenes will make them tense. Why? Because this story is not following the usual rules; this rollercoaster doesn't have safety rails. So, slide this moment into the Opening Image, the Catalyst, or the Fun & Games.

Here are a few examples:

- *Scream* – The unexpected killing of Drew Barrymore's character in the opening scene.
- *Hereditary* – The sudden and brutal death of Charlie, the family's young daughter, in a car accident early in the film shatters any sense of safety and establishes that no character is truly safe from the horrors to come.
- *A Quiet Place* – The unexpected demise of a young boy because of a creature attack.
- *Alien* – The chest-burster scene pushes the boundaries of what is possible and tasteful in a sci-fi horror movie. After seeing that, the audience realizes there are no limits to the horror.

When watching horror, there's actually a comfort when we realize a confident and assured Madman is in control. We surrender to it. We let the rollercoaster do its thing. Be that Madman.

KILL THE COMPETENT

In stories of terror, it's best to take away hope. One way to do that is to set up a competent hero, someone who can stand up to the monster. They're tough, they have skills, they know how to use weapons... then you kill them. Even the toughest of characters can't stand up to the monster. Now, it's up to your less than competent hero... oh, the horror!

Sometimes this is a KILL THE RESCUER moment. Think about when Scatman Crothers shows up to save everyone in *The Shining*. He fights through snow and harsh conditions and just when he's there to save the day... he gets an axe smashed into his chest.

Other times, it's an in-charge character who emerges as a leader with a plan to survive, like Samuel L. Jackson in *Deep Blue Sea* or Michael Biehn's Hicks in *Aliens*, who get taken out early.

In horror, every glimmer of hope should be either a rug pull or an oncoming train. The hero has no choice but to deal with the painful reality on their own.

TWISTED FUN & INSIDIOUS GAMES

The Fun & Games beat should not be fun for the hero. They might get chased by chainsaw killers or find themselves stranded on a desert island or being tortured by Jigsaw. Not fun for them... but fun for us.

Don't get hung up trying to make your Fun & Games light and whimsical and free of tension. The Fun & Games beat is all about tension and dread and terror and scares. Twisted fun! Insidious games!

THE INITIAL PLAN: SUBGOALS OF SURVIVAL

In horror, it's easy to write characters as mere victims, enduring wave after wave of torture and torment. However, compelling stories hinge on heroes overcoming obstacles. All horror is ultimately about survival, and even when escape seems impossible, there should be glimmers of hope.

Survival stories thrive when heroes put themselves at risk in desperate attempts to escape or get help or help others. Heroes should juggle survival, their escape plan, and conflict with other survivors. Survival as a goal is often reactionary, so making heroes active is crucial.

One trick is to give your characters subgoals that serve the larger goal of survival. Here are some **common subgoals** heroes can pursue when the battle for survival kicks in:

- WEAPON OR TOOL ACQUISITION – The heroes attempt to find, create, or secure a weapon or tool they believe will help them fight back, call for help, or escape. The effort to obtain it often comes with significant obstacles, danger, or sacrifice, adding tension and stakes to the story. The weapon or tool itself could be something traditional, like a gun or an axe, or an unconventional object that unexpectedly proves effective.
- DISCOVER THE MONSTER'S WEAKNESS – Characters may try to uncover the weakness or vulnerability of the monster or the supernatural entity they are up against, hoping to defeat or escape from it.

- GET OUT – Characters may explore their surroundings, looking for an exit or a way to escape from the dangerous location they are trapped in.
- LEARN THE LORE – Characters may seek information about the origins, nature, or previous encounters with the monster or threat, hoping to gain insights that could aid in their survival.
- FORM ALLIANCES – Characters may try to team up with other survivors or victims to increase their chances of survival and support each other in their escape attempts. This might even be within a conflict-ridden ensemble of characters.
- SECURE A HIDEOUT OR SAFE SPACE – Characters may try to find, travel to, or create a secure location where they can temporarily hide or fortify themselves against the threat.
- CALL FOR HELP – Characters may attempt to establish communication or find a working phone or radio to call for outside help, such as the police or emergency services.
- RESCUE MISSION – Characters may have a personal connection to someone who has been separated from the group or is in immediate danger, and their subgoal becomes rescuing that person from harm's way.
- SOLVE THE MYSTERY – Characters may seek to uncover the mystery behind the threat they are facing, exploring clues or investigating past events to gain a deeper understanding of the situation and potentially overcome it. Some stories even have a "who done it" where part of the surviving entourage is working under the influence or is connected to the monster.
- MEDICAL ATTENTION – After being victimized by monsters, someone needs immediate medical attention. This usually provides a race against time in the middle of the overall battle for survival.

Great stories are driven by heroes who are smart and resilient and keep trying and strategizing in the face of all this terror. Monsters force our heroes into riskier situations. They give our ensembles dilemmas. And they give us heroes worth cheering for.

Remember to communicate these goals to the audience. The audience should always know your hero's plan. That knowledge aligns us with them psychologically and gives us something to track and root for and stress over.

THE MONSTROUS MIDPOINT

Coming up with the Midpoint for your horror story may be your first big decision. It's the Midpoint that often turns an idea into a fully fleshed-out story. It's a gearshift moment that raises the stakes and makes things even more tense going into the Bad Guys Close In beat and the second half of the story.

While a lot of great guidance has been written about the Midpoint in the original *Save the Cat!* book and elsewhere, and all of it still applies here, there are some additional considerations for horror stories. Let's look at **10 common Monstrous Midpoint ideas**:

1. TICKING CLOCK INTRODUCED – The heroes realize they're running out of time to escape the monster, break free from the house, or survive their ordeal. This ticking clock could take many forms: perhaps nightfall is approaching, and they must survive until dawn; maybe a curse has been introduced with a clear deadline; or an injured character is bleeding out, and they must find help before it's too late. It might even be something as simple yet terrifying as running out of air, fuel, or power. The ticking clock adds urgency to every decision the heroes make, amplifying tension and forcing them into action before time runs out.

2. SEX @ 60 – This term for a "romantic moment or connection" at the midway point originated decades ago, when the standard script was120 pages. Often after a love scene or a kiss or some other moment of intimacy amidst the chaos, the heroes have more to lose as they face the horrors together, knowing their newfound bond may not be enough to keep them safe and may in fact cause them to lose focus on personal survival.

3. WIN THAT STIRS THE MONSTER – The hero gets a win, but their victory draws the attention of the malevolent force, which now targets them with increased ferocity.

4. A STRANGER APPEARS – A newcomer joins the group. It might be a survivor looking for help; it might be a mentor type offering assistance and hope. Often these characters harbor ulterior motives that ultimately put everyone in danger.

5. OUT OF THE FRYING PAN – The protagonists are flushed out of their safe haven—only to discover that the new location is even more

dangerous than their previous one, trapping them in a nightmare from which there seems to be no escape. Sometimes it's retreating to a more confined/smaller space, like if they move from the woods into an abandoned cabin. Or they move from the cabin into the basement.

6. A NEW WAY TO SURVIVE – Heroes uncover a new solution to defeating the supernatural threat, but it requires them to delve deeper into darkness and puts them more at risk.

7. THE BIG PLOT TWIST – A shocking revelation upends everything the heroes thought they knew about the horror they're facing, forcing them to reevaluate their strategies and alliances.

8. A STORY MEETS B STORY – The hero's personal conflicts and relationships intersect with the primary threat, adding layers of tension and emotional complexity to their struggle for survival.

9. REVELATION OF THE MONSTER – Especially in slow burn stories, this can be a moment where the monster fully reveals itself. Maybe it's set loose, maybe it comes out of the shadows, maybe it's discovered that whatever is behind the malice in the Fun & Games is a full-blown monster.

THE INCREDIBLY SHRINKING HOUSE

As your story moves into the second half, you need to keep turning up the heat. One way to increase the pressure is by shrinking the space your characters can move in. The claustrophobia of contracting spaces, with fewer hiding spots and places to run, greatly heightens tension. For example, if the story starts in an abandoned farm, by the Midpoint, the hero might retreat to the farmhouse. By the All is Lost moment, they could be locked in the basement, and by the climax, they might be confined to a closet. Reducing the available space can significantly amplify the tension.

PUNISH THE GUILTY

As Sam Raimi told us, the guilty must be punished. The "guilty" doesn't refer to the monster in this case. Instead, it's usually that jerk who betrayed the group for their own greedy or selfish purpose, or maybe the one that brought about all this monster trouble in the first place—like Burke, the betrayer in *Aliens* who puts corporate profit above human life. In *The Mist*,

Mrs. Carmody's fanatical religious beliefs lead to her being sacrificed by the monsters. In *Carrie*, Carrie White's tormentors meet a devastating demise via Carrie's telekinetic fireworks in Act 3.

This little piece of Mad Science is really a two-fer. Add some "guilty folks" into your story. They always spice things up. Then punish them! The audience will love you for it.

HORROR BEAT HEAD FAKE – USE THE BEATS AGAINST THEM

The *Save the Cat!* beats have been around since the beginning of story. *Save the Cat!* explained them and codified them in an accessible and fun way, but a good story has been around for hundreds if not thousands of years. Even before you learned the *Save the Cat!* beats, you internalized them from years of reading and watching TV and movies. You probably even recognized them as you read. You may or may not realize it, but you expect them while you watch stories.

Good horror stories know you know. Horror stories are based on shock. And there's no better way to shock someone than to know what they're thinking.

Imagine this scenario: We're about 75% through a movie and we're expecting the All Is Lost moment, right? Someone is probably going to die. Someone important. We probably even have a good guess who it is...

Then it happens! One of our favorite characters dies. And we know, the Dark Night of the Soul comes next. It's actually a good time to sneak out to the bathroom in a long movie. Usually, it'll be filled with Oscar®-worthy moments of wallowing and reflection and weeping. It's a dramatic beat where we get to take a breath from the carnage and feel the emotional impact of the horror that the hero has endured. It's the calm before the storm.

Hehehehe.

In a horror movie, you might have to hold your bladder for a little longer.

Because that tragic and shocking death, it's just a head fake. The writers "knew we knew," so right when that typical Dark Night of the Soul wallowing moment is about to begin... BAM! They hit us with an even bigger shock! Something that happens directly to the main hero. Something so horrible it feels like it should be the end of the movie. They tricked us!

But wait... doesn't that break the rules!?!

Hell yeah, it does!

Here's the thing: It's okay to have **extra shocks**. The danger is in having too few. It's cool to have multiple moments that feel like Catalysts or Midpoints or All Is Losts or High Tower Surprises. And sometimes, doing this is exactly what catches the audience off guard—because they're In the Hands of a Madman and anything can happen.

One cool side effect of this technique is that when you do a head fake and trick the audience, they'll give up guessing what's going to happen and tracking the beats. They'll feel like the story is off the rails. Then as long as you can keep delivering the beats, even if they follow the familiar tried-and-true patterns, the audience will feel lost.

Don't Breathe, which we'll fully break down in Chapter 14, exemplifies this. It has a great All Is Lost beat where likable thief Alex is caught and beaten by the killer stalking them. It's a classic All Is Lost moment, leaving us with a Final Girl. Standard horror movie beats would then have her harden and go into warrior mode, but she's grabbed by the monster in the REAL All Is Lost beat, taking the story in a shocking and new direction.

The most common beats you'll encounter head fakes are at the Midpoint, the All Is Lost, and in the end (when the audience thinks the movie is over and all the beats have been delivered—BAM! One more scare!).

There are other head fakes that go beyond the beats. Read on.

HERO SWITCH & HEEL TURN

One interesting phenomenon, occasionally seen in horror movies but rarely seen in other genres is the **hero switch**. The switch happens when the hero character either suddenly dies or makes what us pro-wrestling fans call a heel turn. The **heel turn** happens in movies where the hero is suffering some transformation, be it biological like in *The Fly* or *The Werewolf* or demonic like in *The Shining*.

Killing off a hero is such a gut punch that it usually serves as an In the Hands of a Madman moment. We know what the audience expects. We've set the hero up with a Rooting Resume and Things That Need Fixing. We've made an empathetic connection with them. We can already imagine them bloody and shaking yet transformed at the end of the movie. That's how movies are done after all. Right?

No filmmaker would be unhinged enough to cast Drew Barrymore and then spend 10 minutes of their opening on her only to kill her before we even meet any other characters... would they? No screenwriter in their right mind would spend half their movie following Janet Leigh and asking the question "Will she get away with the robbery?", only to kill her in the shower!

Barbarian did a hero switch and made a splash with its audacious storytelling.

Be cautious with these head fakes. Use them wisely. Rules really aren't rules, they're best practices to deliver on common audience expectations. When you break these so-called rules, there's a cost. Be deliberate and intentional when you do. Be methodical about it and a little insidious.

MY BRAIN IS SCARIER THAN YOUR FX DEPARTMENT

You can't write anything scarier than what my mind can conjure. This is why many movies keep the monster in the shadows for as long as they can.

We've seen almost everything imaginable at this point. *Jaws* accidentally lucked into keeping the monster offscreen. It made the actual scenes of the shark more breathtaking and terrifying. Monsters can be hidden behind curtains of fog or shadow, beneath the surface of the ocean or the ground, cloaked by ghostly invisibility or even by using cinematic tricks like POV.

Keeping your monster hidden taps into the primal fear of the unknown. When the audience fills in the blanks with their worst fears, the terror becomes personal and far more effective. When the audience doesn't see the monster, their imaginations work to fill in the gaps, often imagining something far scarier than any CGI creation.

In filmmaking, not showing the monster is sometimes a budgetary necessity that turns into a creative advantage. Limited resources can lead filmmakers to find innovative ways to suggest horror without expensive special effects. In horror, pure imagination can sometimes be more effective than all the big-budget wizardry you can spend studio money on.

DON'T EXPLAIN EVERYTHING

Horror is about the unexplained. The less you explain, the scarier things are. But not explaining stuff isn't an excuse for creating plot holes or completely punting logic. I suggest that you the writer have an explanation or theory for all of it, just don't feel a need to definitively spell it all out.

Characters might theorize what the monster is or what it's up to, but they're often wrong or their theories are incomplete. The second you explain what's going on in *The Blair Witch Project* or get specific about the demon's plan in *The Exorcist* is when things get artificial. In real life, no one has a clear handle on the supernatural or evil... it's all conjecture and best guesses.

Keep it real, keep it scary, keep it a little vague.

THE FINALE A.K.A. THE FINAL STAND

Most horror movies end with the hero having "tasted blood" and after all the subgoals have failed, whether slow burn or wall-to-wall horror, all Monster in the House stories end with a final showdown, a battle for survival.

The **final stand** typically takes one of the following forms:

- WE HAVE TO KILL IT – In the Break into 3, either a new piece of information or a new realization that the only way to survive is to kill the monster. The Finale then becomes a trap or strategy to slay the beast. In many horror stories, the heroes shift gears from hunted to hunter. This happens in *Nightmare on Elm Street.* Nancy, realizing that she can yank Freddy Krueger out of the dream world, sets traps and plans to confront him in the real world, leading to a climactic battle in her own home. We also see this type of final stand in *Alien, I Am Legend, The Exorcist,* and countless other horror flicks.
- WE HAVE ONE LAST CHANCE TO ESCAPE – In the Break into 3, either a new piece of information offers a way to escape the monster or a ticking clock becomes so urgent that escaping RIGHT NOW becomes the only chance of survival. Examples include *The Mist, Get Out, Dawn of the Dead, The Descent, Train to Busan,* and others.
- WE HAVE TO DEFEND OURSELVES – The monster makes a fierce final push and the only hope is to hunker down and fend it off. Often, this sub-beat can turn into the aforementioned "We have to kill it" sub-beat happening around the High Tower Surprise (which we'll describe in the next few pages). *Shaun of the Dead, A Quiet Place,* or even *Halloween* (when Michael finally brings the attack to Laurie Strode) are examples where Finales are about trapped heroes having to play defense against the monster's final assault.

THE FIVE-POINT FINAL STAND

These final stands break out into a series of sub-beats within the *Save the Cat!* beat sheet, built from several moments and or sub-beats. To help guide you, we have a handy-dandy thing we "Cats" like to call the **Five-Point Finale.** It breaks the Finale into five steps, a good roadmap to create your mini-movie:

1. GATHER THE TEAM – Whether it's a team of many or one, this is the time to gather 'em up.

Plans are laid out now, people suit up or barricade the doors or hand out weapons. The heroes give last-minute "good lucks." Sometimes this is just your hero gathering their courage or resolve to tackle the big moment. Your hero has a goal and a plan to win—be it slay the beast, defend the cabin, or run like hell—and this is the preparation.

2. EXECUTION OF THE PLAN – It's time to execute that plan! Attack the monster! Race to safety. Or keep the monster out one last time! It's an all-or-nothing moment of survival.

3. THE HIGH TOWER SURPRISE – Plot twist! We're writers, which means we must be mean to our heroes, so surprise... the plan does not work! Either the monster was way ahead of the hero or something about the hero's plan just wasn't right. Regardless, hope and enthusiasm are ripped out from under them. In our mini-movie Final Stand, this is a Midpoint and All Is Lost jumbled into one.

4. DIG DEEP DOWN – Now it's time to show that our heroes have transformed since Act 1. This sub-beat reflects on the theme and the Dark Night of the Soul. Our hero has changed and can only win the day because they're a new person. Something about this moment goes beyond plot choices; the path to victory is somehow personal and philosophical.

5. EXECUTION OF THE NEW PLAN – The hero executes the new plan (the one they can only do because of what they've learned) and wins the day.

SOME OPTIONAL BUT COMMON FINAL STAND BEATS

Here are three other mini-beats that more often than not appear during the big mano a monster showdown.

1. THE VICTIM BECOMES THE MONSTER – There comes a point in the story, usually somewhere around or in Act 3, where the hero has just completely had it! Something has changed... and now it's time for the monster to be afraid of *them*. This moment is something we can often see in

their eyes and in their actions. It usually gets a huge pop from the audience, because we've been on the hero's side the whole way and now they've changed and they're going to kick ass.

The conversion usually happens at the Break into 3. Fresh off the whiff of death of the All Is Lost, our hero hardens and knows it's time to go primal. They rip out their shard of glass and all the pain channels into pure rage. They've become monster killers!

Other times, the hero is still focused on survival and the final stand doesn't quite become a Kill the Monster type. In these cases, it's often around the Dig Deep Down beat when the hero realizes that the only way out is to slay the monster.

Commonly, the hero uses the monster's tricks against them. For example, in *A Nightmare on Elm Street*, Nancy lures Freddy into her lair, which is filled with traps and tricks. She's become Freddy. In *Predator*, Arnold uses mud to make himself invisible and sets booby-traps to stalk his prey. In *Scream*, Sidney turns the tables on her killers and stalks them and even uses the phone with the Ghostface voice to taunt them. Usually, these tricks are a mirror image of the monster's own attack methods.

When plotting your hero's final stand, pay close attention to the monster's attack methods. Throughout the story, the hero may have unknowingly learned valuable lessons from surviving these encounters—tactics, weaknesses, or patterns they can now use to their advantage in the final showdown.

2. THE BIG TWIST – Horror Finales often have a big shocking twist. Not all horror stories have the twist and, of course, twists aren't exclusive to horror. Dating back to O'Henry and being carried out through EC Comics and *Tales from the Crypt* and M. Night Shyamalan, the big twist has become pretty common.

Movies like *The Sixth Sense*, *Jacob's Ladder*, *Psycho*, *Saw*, *The Others*, *April Fools Day*, *Sleepaway Camp*, *High Tension*, and *Scream* all deliver a big twist ending. The ending serves almost as a rug pull, putting the audience on even more uncertain territory, breaking their brains one last time before the final credits.

3. THE NOT-SO-SECRET WEAPON – This is a final stand beat that comes from my *Writers/Blockbusters* co-host, Jimmy George (who's one of the best and most sought-after script consultants in the business). If you're stuck on

how to kill the monster, one trick is to plant a not-so-secret weapon earlier in the story. Think of the LOADER in *Aliens* or CROSSING THE STREAMS in *Ghostbusters* or the OXYGEN TANKS in *Jaws*—all not-so-secret weapons that pay off in the end.

The key is how subtly you sneak the secret weapon into the earlier scene. Give the set-up a purpose other than a weapon. Make a joke of it. Use it for a practical way to overcome an obstacle. It's important that it's not presented as a weapon. It should be hiding in plain sight, and it should get a moment of use so we feel like it's been used, so when it comes back we remember and it's a bit of an aha! because it wasn't introduced as a way to kill the beast.

This beat usually appears in one of two places: it can either be a major weapon used in the Execution of the Plan, initially bringing the fight to the monster before the High Tower Surprise... or it can be unveiled as a Plan B during the Execution of a New Plan.

ONE LAST SCARE

You know this one. It's the one where the monster rises for one last scare. Michael Meyers takes five bullets and is lying there dead but suddenly lurches up to attack. It's so cliché that you have to ask yourself, "Should I do it?"

The key to executing this overdone beat... is to *know* what the audience is expecting and use that against them. Maybe you won't do it. Maybe you tease it but bring a surprise attack from somewhere else. Maybe the lead character knows it's coming and somehow subverts it. Maybe it happens, but it's a distraction for the *real* big scare.

Use audience expectations against them. The one last scare usually happens either as the High Tower Surprise or sometimes more effectively as a final surprise even after the whole Execution of the New Plan—as one extra shock showing how relentless and hard to kill the monster is.

FINAL IMAGE: THE EVIL LIVES ON

While it's not in any way a requirement of your story, many horror movies use the last beat or shot of the movie to hint that the evil will return. Michael Meyers goes missing after being shot and falling through the window. Sometimes, the evil continuing makes little sense; think of the hand bursting from the grave at the end of *Carrie*.

But it's such a fun beat. And so hard to resist.

Okay, now that we know all about the Five-Point Final Stand, let's look at an example:

***A Nightmare on Elm Street* – Five-Point Final Stand**

Final Stand Type: WE HAVE TO KILL IT!

Gather the Team: After enduring the death of one too many friends and learning more about Freddy Kreuger's origins and psychopathic motivations, *the Victim becomes the Monster*. Nancy gathers her strength and prepares to confront hat, sweater, and dagger-glove-enthusiast Freddy Krueger, by setting booby traps around the house to challenge him in the real world.

Execute the Plan: Nancy enters the dream world, determined to bring Freddy out into reality, end his reign of terror, and pull him into the real world. She traps him in the basement.

The High Tower Surprise: The police arrive. But we get One Last Scare! Nancy and her father go upstairs to the bedroom and find a burning Krueger smothering Nancy's mom in flames. After dad extinguishes the fire, Krueger and the mom vanish into the bed. When Nancy's father leaves the room, Krueger rises from the bed behind Nancy.

Dig Deep Down: Nancy realizes Freddy is fueled by his victim's terror. She taps into her newfound inner strength and resolve to confront him one last time... by controlling her fear. The *not-so-secret weapon* that she'll use to beat the monster is withholding her fear.

Execution of the New Plan: Nancy turns her back to him and doesn't give him the terrified attention he wants and needs. As he moves to attack her, Freddy weakens and disintegrates.

Final Image: We get the extra Evil Lives On sub-beat. In a scene that may not even make sense thematically or according to the rules of the story, Nancy steps outside to go to school and all her friends and family are alive. Was it all a dream? Nancy gets into Glen's convertible to go to school when the green-and-red-striped top suddenly comes down and locks them in as the car careens down the street. Three girls in white dresses jump rope and chant Krueger's nursery rhyme as Nancy's mom is grabbed by Freddy through the front door window and impossibly pulled through.

Using the Five-Point Final Stand ensures you'll have all the necessary twists and turns a good horror Finale needs, delivering both high tension and a satisfying payoff. It also helps to deepen the character arc, often pushing the protagonist to confront their greatest fears or flaws, and reinforces the story's core theme in a powerful, memorable way.

EXERCISES:

1. Okay, it's finally time! Fill out the 15 beats of the *Save the Cat!* beat sheet for your story. Sometimes it's best to start with a brief description of each beat (1 or 2 sentences). Once you settle on all your beats, you can beef those descriptions up to a synopsis level. But while you're still figuring things out, it's best to keep it brief and disposable.
2. Once you have the 15 beats, expand the Finale into a complete Five-Point Final Stand.
3. Use as many of the optional Mad Science beats and techniques as possible. It might be useful to review this chapter as you work through the beats.

PART 5:
BRINGING THE HORROR – MOVING FROM BEAT SHEETS TO STORY

CHAPTER 13: THE TOOLS OF TERROR

You've plotted out a terror-filled roadmap that has the makings of a tension-filled nightmarish story. Now it's time to bring it to life. While all stories are execution-dependent, horror can live or die on little moments of tension, dread, and terror that aren't found in the beat sheet—the moments of horror that play out second by second on the page.

Unlike other genres, in horror, even a loosely plotted slow burn story can capture the attention of the masses—if it delivers terrifying scenes and leaves its audience with bad vibes. People come for the scares and you need to be a maestro of chills and thrills.

Loosely borrowing from Stephen King's terrific non-fiction book *Danse Macabre*, there are three major tools writers use to orchestrate this tension in their horror stories: **dread**, **scares**, and **gross-outs**.

Let's dig into each one of these tools and figure out why and how we should use them.

DREAD

A good horror story never lets you feel safe. The anxiety is always present. Dread is the sense of foreboding and anticipation of something terrible happening without knowing when or how. It provides that slow burn of tension, keeping the audience on the edge of their seats, and is often the primary tool in psychological horror or suspense-first thrillers.

All good horror relies heavily on dread. In fact, dread is one of the biggest differences between amateur and professional scripts and novels. Amateur works often rush to show the fanged, man-eating monster or gross you out with their big disembowelment-via-lawn-dart scene. They often skip the dread altogether and jump right to visceral and shocking scares. They're not only missing out on a huge ingredient to bring the tension, but also scares without dread aren't as much fun.

Dread is where true tension and unease are layered on moment by moment. It's the tightening of a rubber band—the more you pull and stretch, the more anxious you get waiting for that loud, violent snap. Dread also is essential in those early story beats where not a lot of big scares are happening. Depending on the story, the Set-Up and Debate beats can be injected with dread. In a slow burn story, the Fun & Games and Bad Guys Close In beats might be jam-packed with it.

But really, dread should permeate every corner of your horror narrative. So, let's explore some effective ways to weave it into the fabric of your story.

CREATING DREAD WITH DREAD FLAGS

At the center of its dark heart, dread is a series of subtle warnings that something horrible is about to happen. Sometimes these warnings are noticed by the heroes, other times they're ignored, and still other times they're only noticed by the audience as we watch our heroes strut right into danger with no cares in the world. These story-driven red flags can be used scene-to-scene to create a sense that a large scare is on the horizon, or planted within horror scenes to construct a rollercoaster of dread and scares.

Horror writers stack red flags. They might start with the mysterious car parked across the street. Then move to the unlocked door. Maybe the TV and the power are out. There's blood on the steps that the hero doesn't see. There's broken glass. And on, and on, and on... each little bit signaling the audience to get closer and closer to the scare, to the evil.

I call these red flags... **dread flags**—mostly because I like a good pun as much as a good scare. What follows is a comprehensive list of them. As usual, there's probably more. But if your horror story isn't using at least some of these, you probably need to do a "dread pass." I've broken them down into subsections. Let's do it!

DREAD FLAGS

Danger Zone Flags

- OFF LIMITS – Warnings or threats not to enter certain prohibited places or cross a dangerous line or open mysterious doors. These red flags create a sense of foreboding and unease, as the characters are drawn inexorably toward the forbidden zone.

- ISOLATION – Cellphone coverage goes down, the car won't start, the bridge is flooded, the snowstorm blocks the road, the rescue plane has crashed. Sometimes the trap that you lay down for your house is a red flag.

• TOO FAR FROM SHORE/ENTERING THE KILL ZONE – The realization that the heroes are vulnerable due to distancing themselves from help or stepping into an area we know is a kill zone for the monster. Could be drifting out into the ocean where they can't see the shore, or wandering too deep into the woods, or even just venturing into the shadows of a dark alley.

• NAKED & NOT AFRAID – Removing clothing or disarming of weapons or any other removal of gear makes someone extra-vulnerable to the monsters that lurk about.

• DUMB MOVE – The heroes leave their weapons behind or use up their last bullet or leave a door open or kick the map into the water or take a baseball bat to the radio or get drunk or take a drink of a potion offered to them by a creepy stranger. The dumb moves lead to isolation or deepening vulnerability.

• HELP IS NOT ON THE WAY – We get a glimpse of someone who might represent a savior... but in some way, they're distracted, incompetent, or otherwise questionable.

• WEIRD DREAMS & SURREAL EXPERIENCES – A hero may dream or see ghostly figments of their imagination. These dreams and experiences can be caused by a mental state (disease, injury, trauma, chemicals) or from certain vibes or the haunted nature of a place.

Atmospheric Flags

• ALL TOO PEACEFUL – The atmosphere and vibe are overly peaceful, creating an unsettling sense of calm in the audience before the storm.

• TOO QUIET – An eerie silence or absence of sound can be a red flag in horror movies, creating a sense of unease and tension. This red flag often signals that something is amiss, or that danger is lurking nearby.

• ASSAULT ON THE SENSES – Strange smells, eerie sounds, creepy music, abnormal temperatures, itchy crawling skin—when supernatural entities are at work, they can often assault the senses in unexpected ways. These sensory disturbances can be a sign of something otherworldly.

• HOWLS IN THE DARK – Screams, a monster in the distance, wolves howling at the moon. These sounds can set a creepy tone and foreshadow what's to come.

• ANIMAL ENCOUNTERS/INFESTATIONS – Unusual animal behavior like angry dogs or scarred birds or wildlife gathering. Whether it's a swarm of bees or a colony of spiders, infestations of bugs can also be a sign that something sinister is afoot.

• MARKINGS/SYMBOLS – From mysterious glyphs to satanic symbols, these markings can set an ominous tone and foreshadow what's to come.

• DARK AND/OR STORMY – If it's a Dark and Stormy Night... beware! We all know bad weather brings the monsters.

• LACK OR EXCESS OF LIGHT – This red flag often signals that the characters are in a place where they shouldn't be, or that something is affecting the natural order of things.

• DISTURBING DECOR – Weird or disturbing decorations or artwork or even some otherworldly interior design can create a sense of unease and discomfort.

• SIGNS OF DEATH – Blood, tombstones, rotting plants, maggots in food, and things that remind us of death increase our unease and sense of foreboding.

• DESERTED AND ABANDONED POSTS – When characters encounter a place that is recently or long abandoned... watch out!

• ROTTING – An unnatural, sickly, or decaying appearance of flora or fauna = red flag!

• EYES OFF THE PRIZE – A momentary distraction or vision blocked by something dangerous or a potential place where we know the monster may appear are often red flags.

Evidence of Evil

• OMINOUS EVIDENCE – We all know history repeats itself, especially in horror stories! Often past crimes go unsolved or solved wrongly, which can get the audience thinking.

• CHECKOV'S CHAINSAWS – The discovery of weapons or implements of evildoing create a sense of dread, as the viewer realizes the characters are in mortal danger. A missing knife from the knife block, an empty spot where the chainsaw once hung, or the discovery of a weapon with fresh blood—all hint at imminent danger and raise the tension.

• TECHNICAL DIFFICULTIES – Power failures, cars not starting, phones not working, or other unexplained technical problems. Technology is supposed to make our lives easier, but in horror movies, it's often the first thing to go wrong, leaving us uneasy and vulnerable. From cell phones losing their signal to cars breaking down in the middle of nowhere, technical difficulties can be a major red flag.

• SABOTAGE – Slashed tires, cut power lines, missing stuff. When it's clear that someone or something is trying to harm the protagonists, it's a red flag that things are about to get a lot worse.

• THEY'RE HERE – Voices, apparitions, and supernatural disturbances. Ghosts and other supernatural entities are a staple of horror movies, and their presence can be a major red flag. Sometimes it's even the mention of haunting or magic or something otherworldly. From disembodied voices to apparitions, these disturbances can signal that something evil is at work.

• WHERE'S THE CAT? – Unexplained disappearances of friends, neighbors, or even pets.

• LEFT FOR DEAD – When characters encounter injured or sick or dead strangers... usually victims of the monster.

• HYPE THE HORROR – Someone who has faced the monster gives testimony about just how deadly the force they're up against is.

Cinematic Moments

• CAT-SCARE – Quick jump scares that fake us or the hero out. These allow us (and the hero) to let our guard down. But we've seen enough horror movies to know... the next one will not be a cat.

• KILLER POV – A stalky monster POV of its next victim, sometimes through the eyes of a mask or in some altered monster POV.

• I'LL BE RIGHT BACK – The moment a character heads towards a dangerous location, often to investigate something or fetch an item.

• FLICKERING LIGHT – When the light keeps going in and out, leaving corners of our view in shadow, we know something is hiding there. Could be that flickering bulb or those matches we're using for the light or the flashlight with the dying battery or even waves of dark fog.

• SLOW PACE – When the scene is stretched with barely anything happening except red flags, audiences sense a scare is coming. The lack of cutting a shot can also be a big anxiety-filled tip that something might be coming.

• FOUND FOOTAGE – Flipping to security or body cams or janky audio connections is a cinematic signal that something raw and unfiltered and horrible is about to happen. Our subconscious knows all too well that we never watch raw security cam footage for anything positive.

Provoking the Monster

• SUMMONING THE BEAST – A character does something that will unknowingly attract the monster's attention, creating a noise or a smell or disturbing some magical object with no realization of the horror that might be coming.

• MOCKING THE MONSTER – Characters who blatantly make fun of the monster. We *know* karma will ultimately get them.

Bad Behaviors of Characters

• FREAKY FRIENDLY – Overly friendly people can freak us out. Sometimes the overly friendly character seems like a smokescreen—or there's just something off with their personality.

• SILENT & DEADLY – On the opposite end of the spectrum, sometimes characters are too quiet—either hiding something or sending us dangerous signals.

• BAD TEMPER/VIOLENT TENDENCIES – Some people can't contain their anger. Their outbursts are a ticking clock. We know eventually that same venom will explode and be focused on our heroes.

• OVERSTEPPING – When characters (especially strangers) overstep, pry, or overly insist on something, there may well be secret, darker agendas beneath the surface.

• CREEPY OBSESSIONS – A character has an obsession they perceive as normal, but others think is extremely weird.

• UNWANTED CONFLICT – Unexpected and overblown confrontations or tensions can hint at the promise of more to come.

• STRANGE CUSTOMS – Customs that are mysterious to the hero because they're either foreign, exotic, or just plain odd.

• WHY'S EVERYONE ACTING WEIRD? – The characters behave strangely around the hero, creating a sense of paranoia and unease.

• VIOLATIONS OF PRIVACY – Stalking or spying or going through things. Characters feeling like they're being watched or followed.

Suspense

• BOMB-UNDER-THE-TABLE – Tell the audience something the hero doesn't know. Something dangerous: the killer's in the backseat; the window's wide open; the house is haunted. That the hero is ignoring the danger and is completely vulnerable will drive audience anxiety through the roof.

When using dread, the key is subtlety and variance. These moments usually don't call too much attention to themselves, but if done right they will build that tension in the audience.

While subtle... they're abundant. Scares might only come about once every 10 pages or so, but be sure you have a dread flag on almost every couple of pages or at least one a scene. And sometimes you might have multiple carefully crafted and nuanced dread flags on a single page.

Flags tend to escalate. Much like a rollercoaster climbing its first steep hill, the tension in your story starts slow, each moment clicking into place like the steady clank of the ride's chain pulling the cars upward. At first, the creaks and rattles are distant, almost ignorable. But as the climb continues, the sounds grow louder, sharper, and more frequent, each one a jolt of anticipation that tightens the audience's grip on the safety bar. The pauses between creaks shorten, the air feels thinner, and every second stretches out unbearably as the peak nears. Then, just as the rollercoaster crests the hill, there's a fleeting, weightless silence—a suspended breath—before the plunge. Your scare should hit with that same stomach-dropping force, a sharp release after an excruciating build-up.

SCARES

A **scare beat** is a moment that scares or frightens the audience. These beats can come in a variety of forms and are often timed to occur at specific points throughout the story. I've worked with movie studios that literally would count pages between scare beats (the norm seems to be every 10 pages in a screenplay) and would hire writers to do "scare passes" to add and enhance the scare beats, similar to comedy writers who do "joke punch-ups."

Depending on the story, many of these beats are often followed by moments of intense action. Scares can kick off a big chase or battle or grotesque kill. Once the scare happens, built-up dread and tension are replaced by adrenaline and pulse-pounding thrills.

More scares can happen, but they have to escalate. Each consecutive scare needs to top the previous one. Think of it like a comedian delivering a punchline—if the audience laughs, the comedian might add a quick follow-up joke, called a "tag," to extend the laugh and make it even stronger. In horror, each scare acts as a punchline, and every follow-up scare (or "tag") builds on the last, keeping the tension high and the audience on edge without giving them a chance to fully recover.

Here are several types of **scare beat types**, with examples from popular horror movies:

1. JUMP SCARES – A sudden, unexpected event that causes the audience to jump out of their seats, equivalent to a Boo-Scare we might get at a local Halloween haunt. Examples include the infamous hospital attack in *The Exorcist 3*, the dismembered head in *Jaws*, or the hide-and-seek moment from *The Conjuring*.

2. FAKE SCARES – This sibling to jump scares involves building tension and anticipation, only to reveal that there is no actual danger. Examples include the scene in *Scream* where Sidney is startled by Billy climbing through her window, and the cat jump scare in *Alien* when Brett is startled by Jonesy. These scares also build dread... because we have seen enough movies to know they're red herrings and the real scare is mere seconds away.

3. PSYCHOLOGICAL SCARES – These play on the audience's fears and anxieties based on the context of the story, rather than relying on visual effects. They're also moments where the story shows the audience something and lets us do the math. The participatory nature makes this

type of scare extra potent. Examples include the ending of *The Blair Witch Project*, where Mike is inexplicably standing in the corner paying off a spooky legend, or *The Shining*'s "All Work and No Play" moment.

4. SUPERNATURAL SCARES – These involve ghosts, demons, or other supernatural beings. Examples include the ghostly apparitions in *The Conjuring* and the demon possession in *The Exorcist*.

5. CREEPY KIDS SCARE – These involve creepy or sinister children, often playing off the notion of innocence corrupted. Examples include the twins in *The Shining* and the little girl in *The Ring*.

6. CREEPY ANIMAL SCARES – These involve creepy or sinister animals, such as rats or spiders. Examples include the spider scene in *Arachnophobia*, the rat scene in *Willard*, and the maggots in *The Lost Boys*.

7. BODY HORROR – These involve the destruction or deformation of the human body, often through infection or mutation. There's a fine line between body horror scares and gross-outs, which are covered in the next section. Body horror scares focus on emotional and psychological ramifications of the physical horror more than the shock value of the body transformation. Examples include the transformation scene in *The Fly* and the rotting body parts in *The Substance*.

8. CLAUSTROPHOBIC SCARES – These involve a sense of confinement or claustrophobia, often in tight or enclosed spaces. Examples include the coffin scene in *The Vanishing* and the closet hiding scene in *Halloween*.

9. THEATER OF THE MIND SCARES – These involve using sound effects and other cinematic tricks to let a scare play out in our imagination. Examples include the whispering in *The Grudge* and the eerie sound of children laughing in *The Blair Witch Project*.

10. SUDDEN APPEARANCE SCARES – These scares involve the sudden appearance of a frightening object or entity, such as a monster or a ghost. Examples include the spider-walk scene in *The Exorcist* and the "demon over the shoulder" in *Insidious*.

GROSS-OUTS

Gross-out horror is a special category of scare beats. These shock-value moments inspire disgust and revulsion from the audience. The keys to a good gross-out are:

1. PUSH THE ENVELOPE – Don't play it safe. Gross-outs typically push into uncomfortable... maybe even distasteful... territory. By taking them one step too far, lingering on them for an extra second, or doing something that really makes people want to look away, gross-outs often achieve the visceral impact they need.

2. MAKE THEM SCARE BEATS – Add them to a scare beat for double impact. These are scares that rely on gruesome or bloody visuals to shock and disgust the audience. Examples include the chest-bursting scene in *Alien* and the vomit scene in *The Exorcist.*

3. MOVE THE PLOT – These moments do more than shock and disgust; they signal pivotal shifts or escalations in the story. By intertwining the gross-out with a key moment in the narrative, you can deliver an additional layer of impact to the audience.

4. MAKE IT RELATABLE – Small gross-outs can be more interesting than the biggest acts of violence. Sure, enormous explosions of blood and gore can be shocking... but the personal ones stick. *A Quiet Place* has all kinds of violence and horror, but the one moment that sticks out is when our very pregnant hero slowly steps on a large nail sticking out of the steps and then steps off of it. It's real, it's painful, and it's relatable. We've all felt the pain of stepping on a nail, or a tack, or a Lego. We feel the pain with the hero. And in the theater I saw it in, this moment got the biggest gasp.

5. MATCH YOUR TONE – The tone of your film or story should guide how you use and execute gross-outs. A dark, serious horror film like *Hereditary* will use gross-out moments differently than a horror-comedy like *Evil Dead II.* In a seriously toned story, the gross-out can be more subdued and realistic, adding to the grim atmosphere. The story may hold off on anything too gory until the end and then use the gross-out sparingly, so its impact is greater.

In a more comedic or splatter-fied story, the gross-out might be exaggerated and over-the-top to elicit a mix of horror and laughter. The story might relentlessly throw gross-outs at the audience where they push past the point of shock and into an area where they're meant to amuse or overload the senses.

Gross-outs should complement the overall tone rather than clash with it. If your story is more psychological and slow-burning, a sudden, graphic gross-out can break the immersion if not handled carefully. Conversely, in a high-octane, gore-filled narrative, a lackluster gross-out can feel out of place and fail to deliver the intended shock.

6. CONSIDER CHARACTER KARMA – Gross-out moments can serve as a form of character karma, where the level of gruesomeness reflects the character's actions and choices. For instance, a particularly vile antagonist might meet a horrific and detailed end, satisfying the audience's desire for justice. Conversely, a sympathetic character might be dispatched with more nuance, as the audience's empathy can heighten the impact of the scene.

On the flipside, stories sometimes dispatch a favorite character in the cruelest, most splattery way, just to show that anything can happen and how cruel the story and the storytelling can be. The infamous "Negan moment" in *The Walking Dead*, where Negan brutally murders Abraham and Glenn, is a prime example of pushing the boundaries of gross-out horror. This scene balanced the show's gritty survival tone with a level of graphic violence that shocked and horrified viewers, establishing Negan as a formidable antagonist. While Abraham's death fit the character-karma framework, Glenn's excessively brutal and prolonged demise elicited a strong emotional backlash, risking alienation of the audience. This shocking moment underscored the fine line between impactful storytelling and gratuitous violence, demonstrating the importance of tone and character considerations in extreme horror scenes.

UNCANNY VALLEY

The **uncanny valley** is an unsettling feeling that gets under the skin of your audience. It can be a powerful tool in your horror story.

Imagine something "almost" human. The doll from *M3GAN*. The creepy stuffed clown from *Poltergeist*. Imagine the faceless creepiness of *Slenderman* or the freakishly tall monster in *It Follows* or the weird thing with hands with eyeballs from *Pan's Labyrinth*. It's what makes Michael Myers's mask so creepy and Pyramid Head from *Silent Hill*, the stuff of nightmares. *The Ring* applied the uncanny valley by shooting the ghostly girl walking backward then playing it forward in the actual films. It gave her a weird twitchy walk. Human... but not quite.

These not-quite-human things mess with our brain. We want to make sense of things. Our minds will work overtime to square the circle.

Think about what makes something human and then tweak it a bit... to make it not quite. These touches hit at the audience's subconscious, provoking deeper, unsettling vibes.

NIGHTMARE FUEL

The intent of horror is to scare. But what does that mean? If you imagine telling a ghost story at a Friday night campfire, there are really two types of punchlines:

1. THE OOGA-BOOGA – The Ooga-Booga scare is the jump scare. It's the horrible thing that frightens us in real time as we're experiencing it, causing a primal physical reaction. It's the kid in the mask jumping out at us in Halloween Horror Nights that makes our hearts skip a bit. It's winding someone up like Bill Murray in *Meatballs*, talking about the killer who stalks the woods and flashing the hook in your hand and making everyone jump and scream.

2. SCARES THAT SCAR – These scares follow you home. These horrific moments imprint new anxiety on your brain or throw gas on the fire of terrors you're already worried about. Imagine you're on a camping trip, and just before everyone goes to sleep, someone tells a story about ghosts that haunt the woods and prey on anyone who falls asleep. Then they say "goodnight." This kind of scare lingers, making you reconsider your safety and surroundings long after the story ends, leaving a lasting impression that can make even familiar activities feel terrifying.

If you want to construct a scare that scars, three elements might help:

1. CONFRONTING OUR FEARS AND BELIEFS – This type of residual scare mines the very fears and beliefs that plague your audience's subconscious minds. It exposes the unsettling concepts that keep us awake at night, from the intrusion of a home invader to the eerie specter looming over us as we open our eyes. It taps into the supernatural realms we dare to consider.

For example, Catholics who witness *The Exorcist* confront their faith and deep-rooted fears, while tales of haunted houses like *The Conjuring*, and the UFOs of *Fire In the Sky*, or Bigfoot in *Exists*, blur the lines between the plausible and the paranormal. Mundane killers and creatures from Michael Myers to Cujo feel like they could be based on real horrors that plague our world. The more a story flirts with what "might be real," the deeper the story penetrates our psyche, ensuring that the horrors linger long after the tale has ended.

2. HORROR ON HOME TURF – The goal is to cast a sinister shadow over the everyday, making familiar settings and situations the breeding ground for unsettling thoughts. It's about placing horror in the commonplace elements of life that we all share. Whether it's the menacing clown and the haunted television set in *Poltergeist*, the vast and treacherous ocean in *Jaws*, the innocuous act of camping in *The Blair Witch Project*, or the chilling specter hovering outside the bedroom window in *Salem's Lot*, these examples transform the mundane into the macabre.

3. EVERYDAY QUESTIONS/HORRIBLE ANSWERS –This type of residual scare provides chilling explanations for those everyday mysteries that leave us bewildered. The aim is to lead our minds down shadowy alleys when confronted with the inexplicable—whether it's the eerie noises emanating from the attic, the sudden swing of an unexplained door, or the shattered window. By offering worst-case horror explanations for these enigmas, storytellers ensure that the next time we bear witness to a similar mystery, our minds will take us to eerie and unsettling places.

THE DREAD-O-METER

In any good scare scene, there's a dance of dread and terror. Usually, scare beats are preceded by multiple dread flags. Dread is like inflating a balloon. With each breath, you get closer and closer to bursting. You want to fill your dread balloon to the limit and keep puffing and puffing and puffing until the audience knows it's going to pop. Then puff a little more and a little more until... BOOOOM!

The BOOOM! is a scare or a gross-out.

The scare essentially pops that metaphoric dread balloon right in your audience's face. But now you're back to zero. Now you have to rebuild the dread and pump that balloon up breath by tension-filled breath.

One way to track your dread as you're writing or rewriting is to use a Dread-O-Meter.

The **Dread-O-Meter** tracks where audience tension is on a scale of 0 to 10. As your audience experiences dread in your story, up the meter. Moment by moment, you make the call whether your dread ticks up a point or 2 or 3. When you get to 10... push it a little just to stress people out. Maybe your red zone goes from 8 to 12. Just know that this is the level where people might be looking away from the screen. So, use the red zone wisely!

Let's look at a scene-level example.

Scene: The Clap Game in the Dark from *The Conjuring*

The scene takes place in a haunted house, so some dread is already established. Nothing wildly bad has happened to our heroes, but they're vulnerable and evidence of scary things is all over the place. Because of this, the Dread-O-Meter has already ticked up to about a 2 before the scene even starts. I'll point out the Dread Flag in all caps.

Dread, Scare or Gross-Out	Action/Description	Dread-O-Meter
Dread	Clapping from an empty room. The audience knows this is a supernatural disturbance, even if Carolyn (Lili Taylor) is still on the fence. This is an example of THEY'RE HERE.	3
Dread	Carolyn yells "Who is that?" Nothing answers. She heads toward the danger. (two red flags here: ALL TOO QUIET and I'LL BE RIGHT BACK)	4
Dread	She moves deeper and deeper into the house, chasing the source of the sound (DRIFTING AWAY FROM SHORE). Then the door is opened behind her...	6

Dread, Scare or Gross-Out	Action/Description	Dread-O-Meter
Dread	Carolyn goes into the basement! ENTERING THE MONSTER'S KILL ZONE.	7
Dread	Just as she retreats, the door slams in her face and she falls to the bottom of the steps! It's a scare, so it kills some of the dread in gasping relief, but it also is a new escalation. She's TRAPPED IN THE KILL-ZONE.	8
Dread	A ball bounces out from a pile of junk (SUPERNATURAL DISTURBANCE). Then as Carolyn sprints away, the lightbulb bursts, leaving her in total darkness. (TECHNICAL DIFFICULTIES)	9
Dread	Now, Carolyn can only use matches to see. (FLICKERING LIGHT)	10
Scare	The Dread-O-Meter is off the charts before CLAP-CLAP! A ghostly pair of hands claps behind her head terrifying us! (SUDDEN APPEARANCE SCARE)	1

Here's another scene. This one from *Jaws*:

Scene: The Cold Open – Chrissy's Death

The scene takes place on the beach at dawn. Chrissy runs off alone for a swim. A guy chases after her, but he's a little too drunk to swim.

Dread, Scare or Gross-Out	Action/Description	Dread-O-Meter
Dread	Chrissy heads toward the Ocean. It's DARK AND STORMY since we know night brings danger. She strips off her clothes in a dread flag of NAKED & NOT AFRAID.	2
Dread	SHARK POV (KILLER POV) in the water. Uh-Oh!	3
Dread	Chrissy jumps into the ocean (INTO THE KILLZONE).	5
Dread	Chrissy's friend passes out on the beach. (HELP IS NOT ON THE WAY)	6
Dread	Chrissy swims out deeper into the calm waters. (TOO FAR FROM SHORE)	7

Dread, Scare or Gross-Out	Action/Description	Dread-O-Meter
Dread	Another SHARK POV (KILLER POV) underneath Chrissy swimming. Moving up toward her legs.	8
Scare	On the water's surface, Chrissy is jolted by something tugging on her legs. The release of the scare drops the meter down a bit (but not all the way).	4
Scare	Chrissy is dragged side to side, thrashing and screaming for help, powerless to escape the shark that has her legs under the water. This second scare drags the meter down even further.	2
Dread	Chrissy's friend is still passed out on the beach. (HELP IS NOT ON THE WAY)	3
Scare	Chrissy screams, "It hurts!" as the shark continues to drag her left and right on the surface of the water.	2

Dread, Scare or Gross-Out	Action/Description	Dread-O-Meter
Dread	Chrissy grabs a floating buoy and gets a moment of relief. (ALL TOO CALM)	3
Scare	Chrissy's ripped away from the buoy, screaming and thrashing, and pulled under the surface never to be seen again.	1
Gross-Out	Blood in the water. Pure climatic release. We're no longer worried... we're shaking!	0

What's instructive from the above scene breakdowns is just how much winding of tension plays into a scare scene. The most important takeaway is to go beyond just a quick scare. Milk the tension. Pull that rubber band to the breaking point, until we're plugging our ears and squeezing our eyes shut, knowing what's about to happen.

Your scare scenes are the money of your story. Take the time to map them out with a Dread-O-Meter to make sure you're fully milking them for all their terror juice!

SCARES PER PAGE

I recently talked to a big-shot horror producer who said they were looking for movies with 4 BIG scares. One in Act 1. One in Act 2a (before or at the Midpoint), one in Act 2b (after the Midpoint), and one in Act 3.

Take this advice for what it is: one producer's magic formula for Hollywood-level horror projects. Maybe A24 or Indy producers or even another studio might be different.

But it might be interesting to ask yourself, what are your story's four big scares?

First off, what's meant by a **big scare**? I interpret this as a set piece that has at its centerpiece a memorable scare that moves the plot forward. Think of the shower scene in *Psycho*, the blood test scene in *The Thing*, the opening disastrous trip to the drugstore in *A Quiet Place*, or the final chase and confrontation in *Get Out*.

These big scares happen around the single-scene beats of the beat sheet. Act 1 might have a big opening scare or might shock us at the Catalyst or show just how deadly the problem is in the Break into 2.

Act 2 often has some wiggle room depending on the story to deliver a big scare in the Fun & Games. The Midpoint and the All Is Lost are also ideal moments for other big scares.

Usually, Act 3 is one big scare-fest. Sometimes at the High Tower Surprise of the Finale... you reveal one last shocking surprise that people will still be shaking about as they leave the theater.

It's okay to have more than four big scares. But it's probably smart to make sure you have at least four that are driving the plot, forcing character decisions, or taking players off the board. In other words, your beat sheet should specifically mention at least 4 scares, spread out over your story.

EXERCISES

1. After you have a pretty solid beat sheet for your story, making sure you're delivering the maximum amount of dread and scares is the next step.

   Referencing the dread flags section of this chapter, go back into your beat sheet and add descriptions (or even notes for later) about how you can incorporate as many dread flags as possible into your story. Dread is especially important early on before the battle for survival takes over, once you get to that point where the narrative can survive more off thrills and adrenaline. Before that, make sure you're loading up on the dread.

   Identify your scares and gross-outs. Can you add more? Do you have enough? Are they spaced out enough to satisfy your fright-hungry audience?

2. Identify your big scares or horror set pieces. Make sure you have at least 4 scares. Write a Dread-O-Meter for each of these scares.

CHAPTER 14: TWO HORROR CASE STUDIES

Here are a pair of beat sheets to bring everything we've done together. We'll also go beyond the beats to see how the dread flags and mad science techniques play out. And I'll call out some techniques in the descriptions of plot. We'll start with a relentless horror example (*Don't Breathe*) and then finish up with a slow burner (*Get Out*).

Don't Breathe **(2016)**
Relentless Horror Example
Monster in the House Subgenre: Escape the Lair

Monster (PSYCHO KILLER): The Blind Man. A blind war vet, shattered by the death of his daughter. The grief and unjustness have transformed him into an unrelenting monster. He's a monster with reasons. Often the scariest kind.

House (IMPRISONED): The locked-down house of our monster: a makeshift prison

Sin (ARROGANCE): The death of the Blind Man's daughter by a rich person who got away with it brings about the monster's unhinged need for justice. It's a similar "unfairness" that leads to the main character's sins of GREED and TRESPASSING as she feels ARROGANTLY entitled to the things she steals.

Don't Breathe was a sneaky hit. Around the time when the Home Invasion genre was getting some juice, it flipped the script, setting the invaders as the heroes and the invaded as the monster. The story is fast, relentless, and shocking. It's also one of those rare films that quickly became a comp for every studio that did horror or thriller. At every general I'd hear: "What we'd really like is another *Don't Breathe*!"

In my time, a handful of other movies had this "We'd like another" influence on the town: *Taken*, *John Wick*, and *Get Out* come to mind. What do all these flicks have in common? They're primal, simple to pitch, kind of timeless (even if they speak to politics or society of the times), and they're inexpensive.

And all of them are structured so well, they're worth studying.

Opening Image/Opening Scare: From high above, we zoom in on an urban landscape. We lock on a mysterious man, our monster, the Blind Man, dragging a bloody body down a street in the middle of the day. The dead girl is our hero. It's an In the Hands of a Madman moment. The filmmakers have literally killed off the lead in the opening seconds of the movie!

Of course, it's a flash forward. So, the question is: how do we get there? The flash forward is risky. This one is so quick and spoil-ery, I wonder if it was a post-production decision maybe after a test screening or something. It definitely plants a lot of audience superior suspense and dread on the table for better or worse.

Set-Up: We meet our hero, Rocky, and her two cohorts (Alex and Money) doing their thing: they rob rich people's houses. Alex is the nice guy who has a crush on her and also has a dad who installed the security system at the property.

During the robbery, we see Rocky trying on fancy clothes and laying in an expensive bed. She wants to leave the mean streets of Detroit and find something better. A young woman with a dream. Classic Rooting Resume stuff.

Theme Stated: Rocky longs to move to California with her younger sister, Diddy, and escape a terrible home life with an abusive deadbeat mother and her crappy alcoholic boyfriend. Stealing things isn't getting them the money they need. They need to steal cash. At one point she says: "Some things you can't change. No matter how unfair." This unfairness is at the heart of the story. It drives the monster and our heroes in flawed quests to make things right.

Catalyst: Money gets a tip on a new potential target from their fence. Gulf War veteran Norman Nordstrom has $300,000 in cash in his house in an abandoned Detroit neighborhood. It was reportedly a settlement after a wealthy young woman, Cindy Roberts, killed Norman's daughter in a car accident.

Debate: Should they rob this guy? It's risky. Not like other jobs. And the amount of money rises to the level of larceny. Alex's father can get into huge trouble. The amount of cash means it might be their last job. But Alex refuses to do it. He's the voice of reason and knows it's a bad idea.

Rocky begs him for help as Alex gathers more information about the potential target. He does some final research... and it's game on.

They scout out the building. It's the only occupied house within a few blocks. A vicious dog attacks their car. They realize the target is a shut-in; they'll have to do the job while he's still in the house. Then they spot him. He's blind. He lost his sight in the war. It seems wrong, but they're going to do it, anyway.

But can they get in?

Breaking into the house is filled with dread. The house is isolated. It's dark and ALL TOO QUIET. The ex-war veteran is a paranoid type. He's changed the locks, and barred the windows, and there's the guard dog and other stuff going on. This "easy job" might not be as viable as they think.

Rocky spots a window on the second floor and climbs up. It's an ENTERING THE KILLZONE moment of dread. She breaks the glass window... ALL TOO LOUD. Alone, she navigates the house. We spy some DISTURBING DECOR (the house is a mess; the pictures are upside down).

We linger on sharp and ominous tools, CHEKOV'S CHAINSAWS that will come into play in a brutal way later. There's even CINEMATIC DREAD... a single uncut shot tracking them through the creepy dark house.

Then they hear some Creepy Music. Money checks it out, entering the Blind Man's bedroom and using gas to knock him out.

Break into 2: Rocky finds the safe. They debate how to open it. Money has brought a gun (DUMB MOVE). He wants to shoot the safe (DUMBER MOVE). Alex wants to leave. Rocky is in the middle. But Money shoots the lock in a SUMMON THE BEAST moment that crosses the line. Alex decides to leave. He tries to take Rocky with him. But her desperation and flawed thinking are too strong. She stays for the loot. Alex heads for the door, leaving Rocky alone with an unhinged Money.

B Story: The relationship between Alex and Rocky highlights the theme. It's almost a two-hander through most of story. Alex is the nice guy and feels the most morally sound. He's already on his way toward a character arc and someone who wants Rocky to change for the better. At one point before they break in, he asks Rocky about her ladybug tattoo. She describes a story about how after her dad died, her mom would lock her in the trunk of her car and a ladybug once visited her keeping her company.

Alex tells her he's going to California with her. The two have a deeper connection and empathy beyond crime. Alex has a crush on her. And Rocky, well, she feels comfortable enough to be vulnerable with him.

Fun & Games: The Blind Man appears behind Money. Now the story evolves into: What to do? How to survive? After a tense standoff, the Blind Man attacks him and chokes him to death. He kills Money in a KILL THE COMPETENT moment. (Money was the most hardened and armed among them.) Alex, having heard the gunshot, doesn't leave and moves to find Rocky. Rocky—stunned—ends up in a closet, frozen.

What follows for the rest of the movie's 90-ish minutes is a nonstop RELENTLESS HORROR sequence of survival horror. Our blind war vet goes into monster mode, locking down the house. But Rocky hasn't learned anything. Instead of bolting for the exit, she still wants the money. With her friend dead, she spies the monster opening the safe and sees the combination. Alex and Rocky ultimately regroup and instead of calling the cops, they collect the cash. Now they need to find a way out.

Their first subgoal: the cellar is the only way out. Can they get there? The Monster has a gun, but he's blind. He compensates for his disability with heightened senses and cunning. After several suspenseful close encounters with the stalking killer, they get to the cellar and make their way to the doors to escape.

Midpoint: In a development common to the Escape the Lair subgenre, the story of our monster is deepened when our heroes discover a female prisoner tethered to a rope in the basement in a padded room, almost like a dog on a leash. She begs for help, but they don't have time. Still Rocky—a hero at heart—is stirred. She realizes the girl is the one who killed the daughter. Rocky, probably thinking back to her own time as a prisoner in the trunk of her mom's car, feels a need to save her. But this *raises the stakes*. Not only do Alex and Rocky realize they're dealing with a complete madman, but they're also wasting precious time when they could be getting out of there.

Bad Guys Close In: To make matters worse, the monster has heard the prisoner girl's squeals. Now he's coming for them. They free the girl and start hurrying for the cellar door. They open the door, but the monster is standing outside with a gun. He shoots Alex and the girl. The girl dies.

The story uses THE INCREDIBLY SHRINKING HOUSE technique, trapping them in the claustrophobic basement. The monster cries over the fact he's killed the girl, upping his rage. NOW IT'S PERSONAL.

The Blind Man shuts off the house's power, essentially evening the odds. Now they're in his world!! After a deadly cat-and-mouse stalking sequence where they barely survive, Alex and Rocky escape to the light of the upstairs. But the big killer dog is there! Holy Cujo! The dog chases them up the stairs and they lock themselves into an even SMALLER ROOM. "We're trapped in here," Alex says.

Their subgoals shift to signaling 911 with the alarm remote. Alex just has to get close enough to the remote. But Rocky doesn't want to do it. She still needs that money. The killer is at the door trying to get in. Rocky crawls through the air ducts (the house shrinking smaller and smaller) as the Blind Man breaks in and the dog pushes Alex out the window. He lands on some glass ceiling windows of the lower level, unconscious. Meanwhile, the dog races into the ductwork, chasing Rocky. The ductwork collapses into a tunnel leading back to the basement, sending Rocky down hard.

Alex falls through the glass back into the house. He's still working the subgoal of getting close enough to signal 911. The bad guy is on his tail, shooting at him. They end up in a brutal fight. The Blind Man finally deactivates the remote (so much for 911!) and kills Alex.

Rocky flutters back to life, battered and broken from the fall. Tears in her eyes, she wills herself to move. As she tries to make her way out, the monster grabs her.

All Is Lost: The Blind Man finds Rocky and knocks her out. She wakes up in the basement prison, having replaced the prisoner girl from earlier, tied up like some serial killer's pet.

Dark Night of the Soul: Rocky begs for help. They have a conversation. In an IN THE HANDS OF A MADMAN MOMENT that pushes at the boundaries of "good taste" and "comfort zones," we realize the monster's plan. To replace his daughter, he wants to inseminate Rocky with a turkey baster and have her give birth to his child.

Break into 3: But wait... Alex is alive! Barely. He gears up to go on a rescue mission. Alex attacks the Blind Man. Knocks him out. And frees Rocky. She beats the crap out of the Blind Man. They escape.

Finale:

Five-Point Final Stand

1. **Gather the team:** Rocky wants to call the cops, but Alex won't let them. They have a choice: take the money and run or bring the monster to justice. They take the money!

2. **Execute the Plan:** As they leave, the monster rises and shoots Alex, killing him. Now it's Rocky—the true Final Girl—who is on the run with the dog chasing after her. The isolated neighborhood, once a positive, is now a kill zone. She escapes to the car and the trunk becomes the first NOT-SO-SECRET WEAPON! She traps the dog in the trunk.

3. **High Tower Surprise:** The Blind Man grabs her and drags her back to the house. (This is the scene from the Opening Image.)

4. **Dig Deep Down:** She's dumped inside. She sees Alex lying dead next to her. She says "sorry" to him. It seems she's alone and done. But then, a ladybug crawls over her hand. It's an emotional moment and a reminder of the warrior she's always been.

5. **Execution of the New Plan:** She takes the remote from Alex's hand and hits the alarm. It calls 911 but more importantly, squeals loudly. Rocky's tasted blood. She's a warrior now. While the Blind Man is distracted by the blaring alarm, she beats him silly and he falls hard into the basement. He seems dead... heh....

Final Image: Diddy and Rocky are at the train station on the way to their new life in California. **BUT THE EVIL LIVES ON...** Rocky sees a news report revealing that the Blind Man is alive and has reported nothing stolen. This buys her silence, as she realizes he's letting her live despite knowing she's complicit. In choosing to stay quiet, she acknowledges the unfairness of the world she despises, allowing the evil to continue. Like it or not, she's now part of the same system she resents, and the evil prevails.

Get Out
Slow Burn Horror Example
Monster in the House Subgenre: Final Dude Out of Water

Monster (CULT): The southern white community with a dark secret
House (STRANGER IN A STRANGE LAND): The small town of white folks
Sin: (COMPLACENCY) A modern culture that allows subtle slights and racism to go by without speaking up and demanding better

Opening Image/Opening Scare: An African-American man, Andre Hayworth (the name will be important, much later) wanders lost through an upscale suburban neighborhood at night, searching for a house while talking on a phone. He "sticks out like a sore thumb" and feels uneasy walking around all alone. Suddenly, a sports car pulls up. The driver, wearing a knight's helmet, attacks Andre and dumps him in the trunk. As Opening Scares goes, this is a FIRST KILL or, more specifically, the "last kill" before the monster is brought into a collision course with our hero. It'll be the last real scare we get for a while, so it's strategically placed here to put us at ease that this is indeed a horror movie and one that has a thematic racial component at its heart.

Set-Up: Our hero, Chris, and his girlfriend Rose are getting ready for a trip to visit Rose's family. Chris wonders if Rose even told the family he was Black. He's worried about being the only Black person there, but Rose sets him at ease and assures him her family will love him. The two of them are funny and charming. They're also supportive of each other and smart—a couple we can really root for, which is sometimes rare in horror.

This is a slow burn story, but Jason Blum produced this movie, and this might just be the place he learned to "make sure the drama works even without the horror." Chris and Rose make a cool couple and the plot of this modern-day *Guess Who's Coming to Dinner* is entertaining—even without the big Opening Scare that's set an expectation that the horror will be unleashed somewhere in the second act.

Theme Stated: Rose assures Chris that her parents are not racist and promises that she wouldn't be bringing him home to them if they were. This question is at the heart of the story. People may say they're not racists and even say they would have voted for "Obama for a third term if they could" ... but does that mean the world is no longer racist? Should we just go along with these assurances despite warning signs of what might be beneath the surface?

The drive to the house cuts through the woods (ISOLATION) and when Chris phones his TSA buddy, Rod, on the way, there are even humorous dread flags coming like "Never meet a white girl's parents" (MOCKING THE MONSTER).

Catalyst: In a sudden scare on the drive, Rose smashes into a deer that leaps onto the road. The dying deer serves as a two-for-one dread flag (an ANIMAL ENCOUNTER and a SIGN OF DEATH). Chris approaches it and almost has a deep mystical connection with the animal. We'll discover this accident also harkens back to Chris's *shard of glass*: when Chris was a child, his mom was hit by a car and killed, dying on the side of the road. When a police officer asks for Chris's ID, Rose defends him, but it reveals the underlying racial tensions of where they're going and plants the seed that maybe Chris's apprehension is more right than wrong... despite Rose's reassurances. The encounter with the cop is an UNWANTED CONFLICT hinting at what's coming. The incident plants a seed of doubt in Chris's mind and stirs memories related to his deeper flaw.

Debate: Chris meets Rose's welcoming parents. They're very hip and the vibe is overly friendly, which is a flag unto itself (FREAKISHLY FRIENDLY). Chris gets a tour of the house. Rose's neurosurgeon dad, Dean Armitage, almost makes a point of being non-racist with the photos that hang on the walls and pointing out his racist father's past (OVERSHARING). There's a throwaway line that mentions the locked-off basement (OFF LIMITS) and how the door is sealed and there's mold. The dad points out how there's not another house around for miles away (ISOLATION). Uh-oh. But most off-putting are the two African-American house staff. It's weird enough that the only two Black people around are "the help," but the duo are quiet and very odd (SILENT & DEADLY). Chris immediately clocks it. Something weird is afoot.

Missy, Rose's mother, offers to hypnotize Chris to help him quit smoking. It's a hint of something "otherworldly" (THEY'RE HERE) and he declines. While they talk, Georgina, the mysterious Black woman who works at the house, disturbingly overfills Chris's glass, staring off into nowhere. What's going on? It's a bit of Uncanny Valley. Are these people hypnotized?

Later, at dinner, Rose's brother Jeremy arrives. Jeremy's a loose talker who takes the conversation in uncomfortable directions, like how Chris would make a good wrestler and wants to fight him at the dinner table (OVERSTEPPING). Chris has been clocking all this weirdness. But as is common in a Final Dude Out of Water story, Rose smooths things over by confirming his suspicions, attributing the problem to a subtle ignorance and racism which she's embarrassed about, but she chalks it off to be ultimately harmless.

Unable to sleep, Chris has a mysterious encounter with the two houseworkers. First, in a shocking moment, the male worker sprints at him in the middle of the night and runs right past him without a word. Then Chris sees the woman checking herself in her mirror and strangely primping her hair. He knows he's in some weird territory now, but refuses to say anything to Rose. His own denial fuels the slow burn. He knows something, but he'd rather keep his opinions to himself than stir something.

Break into 2: Missy finds Chris after the encounter and, noticing he's a bit shaken, sits him down. She pries about Chris's smoking and even Chris's mother's death (more OVERSTEPPING). Using her teaspoon, she magically hypnotizes him. Missy tells him to sink into the floor. He has a dream of floating/sinking... and he visits the Sunken Place (WEIRD DREAMS & SURREAL EXPERIENCES WARNINGS).

B Story: Under Missy's spell, he confesses that when he was a kid he ignored the fact that his mother didn't come home because if he called someone, it would "make it real." Later it's revealed that after the hit and run that killed his mom, she lay there beside the road and he did nothing. If he had called 911 or gone to look for her, maybe things would have been different. It's similar to his failure to act throughout the movie. As if silence is easier than calling out a problem. It's a deeply buried *shard of glass*, but through the course of events, he will "taste blood and become a man."

Fun & Games & More Debate: The slow burn Fun & Games is a Fun & Games & More Debate section. Chris doesn't have an overt goal, he has a major question: What the hell is going on here? He senses a monster at play. The Fun & Games becomes a probing beat, filled with subtle mysteries and questions. Chris's eyes are open and his ears are perked for confirmation that something's up.

He wakes up in his bed with his phone unplugged (SABOTAGE). He wanders around continuing to observe the unusual behavior of the two Black houseworkers. He has an awkward chat with the male worker, who acts flat-out BIZZARE, giving more Uncanny Valley vibes as if he's possessed or hypnotized or something.

At a daytime party, the odd neighbors come and give way too much attention to Chris (more FREAKISHLY FRIENDLY), also saying overtly racist things and appraising him like a novelty item. There's lots of OVERSTEPPING and other dread flags as the weirdness seems to escalate. Chris also meets a Blind Man who is overly familiar with Chris's work as a photographer. The encounter seems odd and suspicious.

Midpoint: Chris spots a lone Black man at the party. He approaches and when the man turns, we see that it's the abducted man from the opening, but he's talking strangely. His older white wife quickly ushers him away. Chris thinks he recognizes the man (but can't remember) and realizes all of this is too weird. It's not yet a battle for survival, but it's trending in that direction.

Bad Guys Close In: The slow burn ramps up. The monster—while not completely revealed—becomes more overt. As Chris walks past the talking guests, the camera and the POV linger, giving us a SCARES IN THE SHADOWS moment that Chris isn't privy to: all the guests fall silent in unison and secretly spy on him with their ears. The guests are conspiring in some way.

Back in his room, Chris finds his phone unplugged again (SABOTAGE). When Chris tells Rose his suspicions, he still doesn't quite speak his truth, instead saying that Georgina is messing with him because she doesn't like the fact he's with a white girl. Rose rolls her eyes at all this. Then Chris calls his TSA buddy Rod and clues him into all the strange occurrences. With Rod, he's more honest, which tells us he's holding back with these others in their world.

The weird party's off-kilter attention and unsettling encounters reach a boiling point when Chris sneaks taking a photo of the unusual Black guest and it triggers him to attack Chris shouting, "Get out!" Chris gets more gaslighting as everyone at the party seems to think it's no big deal and explains it away as a seizure. Chris knows it's not a seizure. He finally confesses to Rose his thoughts about the unusual guy who attacked him. He speculates that the weirdness is related to Missy's mystical hypnosis or something. Chris tells Rose he needs to go. Meanwhile, we get another SCARES IN THE SHADOWS scene, as a silent auction with Bingo Cards is happening back at the party—with a large picture of Chris showing that he is, in fact, being auctioned off.

Rose and Chris return to the house and everyone is acting like nothing's weird, all too FREAKISHLY FRIENDLY. Rod calls and confirms that he knows the Black man at the party is, in fact, Andre, a guy who never dressed like that in his life. But just when they're putting all the wild pieces together, the phone goes dead (TECHNICAL ISOLATION).

Chris is done. He and Rose decide to leave right away.

All Is Lost: Then, the BIG TWIST: Chris finds pictures of Rose being friendly with several Black men like himself that look like boyfriends... and two pictures include the two workers looking normal and friendly—nothing like the weird soulless robots they've become. As Chris tries to escape, the family stops him. The lies are over. Missy uses her "hypnosis spoon" to make a sound that knocks Chris straight out (sending him to the Sunken Place). Like all horror movies, this story is now revealed to be one of survival. We knew all along... but now, so does Chris!

Dark Night of the Soul: Chris awakens in the supposedly locked-off basement, which is like a museum with outdated décor, an old-style TV set, bocce balls, and a mounted moose head. Chris is bound to a leather chair. He struggles against it with no luck. He's helpless and trapped.

The old television flickers to life. The curtain is pulled back on everything that's going on. Dean's father, Roman Armitage, has come up with a procedure to achieve immortality. A process that needs bodies... Chris's body!

Meanwhile, Rod takes the case to the cops. They laugh and mock him. He's getting the same gaslighting that's at the heart of this whole damn affair. Rod's on his own. It's up to him to save Chris. He finally gets a hold of Rose on his phone. She crafts a lie about how Chris took off days ago and left behind his phone. Then tries to spin it that Rod is in love with her. Rod sees right through her. She's crazy.

Back in the basement prison, Jim Hudson, a blind art dealer, appears on the TV. He talks directly to Chris. He lays out the dark secret. The white people at the party are part of a group that have had their consciousnesses transferred into a new body. They're essentially stealing Chris's body (as they did the workers and Andre). A part of Chris will still be in the body, but be trapped in the Sunken Place.

Break into 3: Chris is finding his inner warrior. He claws at the armrests (something he has a habit of doing from giving up cigarettes). He digs out some cotton and gets an idea of how he can make his escape.

Finale:

Five-Point Final Stand

1. **Gather the Team** – Rose's brother, Jeremy, arrives to take Chris to brain surgery. Chris pretends to be hypnotized but then brains Jeremy with a bocce ball. He's tasted blood and is in warrior mode. He looks over at that moose head to prepare for his big escape.

2. **Execute the Plan** – Chris fights his way out. He stabs Dean with the antlers. Dean stumbles into the surgery room and knocks over a candle, igniting a fire! Chris heads upstairs where he grabs his phone. Chris battles through Missy and then Jeremy—who comes back for more—but dispatches them brutally.

3. **High Tower Surprise** – Chris zooms away from the burning Armitage house. As he calls 911, Georgina appears in the headlights. He hits her. Shit.

4. **Dig Deep Down** – He looks back. He's a changed man, after all. He can't just leave Georgina lying on the road (like his mother). This is personal now. It's emotional. He won't be paralyzed by fear any more.
5. **Execution of a New Plan** – Chris metaphorically rips out his *shard of glass* and goes back to save Georgina. Together they drive off.

Writer/Director Jordan Peele knows *Save the Cat!* (he wrote a movie, *Keanu*, all about saving a cat) and more importantly, he knows we know it. So, he does a HORROR BEAT HEADFAKE and gives us all the beats before he delivers ONE LAST SCARE.

Turns out Georgina is Rose's grandmother. And she attacks Chris!!!! The car smashes into a tree. As things settle and Chris scrambles to get away, Rose appears ready to kill him with a shotgun. She tells Walter (who is Rose's grandfather) to get him. He charges but Chris—using a NOT-SO-SECRET WEAPON—flashes him with a camera flash, causing him to snap out of it for a second. Bringing the real Walter momentarily out of the Sunken Place. Rose comes up to him with the gun. Walter insists on shooting Chris himself. But surprise! Walter shoots Rose and then kills himself, not wanting to go back to being the Armitage's puppet anymore. Rose is dying. Chris wants to finish this once and for all. He starts to strangle her. He stops short. He's a warrior, but he's not like them. Lights flash. A police car approaches. Rose already is faking, like she's been attacked. But it turns out it's a TSA car... it's Rod! He gets Chris in the car and they ride off.

Final Image: Inside the car, Chris is bloodied... and transformed. He's found his inner strength and his inner warrior. As they drive off, he'll never be the same.

Rose stares off... still alive... the EVIL LIVES ON...

CHAPTER 15: MAKING IT IN HORROR

One of the things I love about horror is that a lot of the creators started as fans of the genre. They were oddballs who built haunted houses and shot gorefest home movies and went to conventions to get Bruce Campbell to sign their chainsaw... just like me.

Because of this, the community is accessible. The horror producers and creators I've met are special. They're different. They are "us" and they haven't forgotten it.

DIY APPROACHES TO YOUR HORROR CAREER

One of the least helpful answers to "How do I break into Hollywood?" might be "Write a great script."

Second on that list might be, "Make your own movie!"

But for a lot of horror goofs like me, the DIY thing is not the worst advice. For some of us, it's often the goal. We grew up dabbling with latex makeup and squirting blood through super soakers and spent our falls wandering around Spirit Halloween stores scouting for props. We're wired different.

If you're part of this tribe, this chapter is aimed at you.

I got my start by writing screenplays I planned to make myself. My first one was a self-produced schlockfest called *Two Front Teeth*, a Christmas horror movie that was a bit like the low-budget Troma films I adored. Despite my "first time director" skills, I still get people who come up to me and ask about that film. And I still have friends and colleagues that I met working on that thing. It ignited a bit of a fire for getting things done and a love of making horror that has kept me going for into three decades now.

The director of *Don't Breathe*, Fede Alvarez, broke into the industry through a combination of talent, determination, and resourcefulness. Alvarez gained widespread attention with his short film *Panic Attack!* (*Ataque de Pánico!*) in 2009, which he made on a shoestring budget of only $300. The duo Adam Wingard and Simon Barrett, known for their work on *You're Next* and *The Guest*, gained recognition through their early DIY horror films. Similarly, Mike Flanagan, director of *Oculus*, first made a version of the film as a low-budget short in 2006, using the same resourceful approach before expanding it into the full-length feature that launched his career in supernatural horror.

Long before that, many old guard horror guys did the same. Sam Raimi kickstarted *The Evil Dead* with a short "prototype" and financed the full-blown movie by hitting up local dentists for money. Peter Jackson, renowned for *The Lord of the Rings* trilogy, started his career kind of mimicking Raimi's game plan with low-budget DIY stuff. James Wan, co-creator of *Saw*, similarly used a short film to showcase the concept and secure funding for what became a massive franchise in the horror world. Frank Darabont got his start by directing a Stephen King "Dollar Baby," using one of King's short stories for just $1—a unique opportunity King offered to young filmmakers. And beyond breaking in, some of the highest-grossing horror films, like *The Blair Witch Project* and *Paranormal Activity*, were made on shoestring budgets by indie filmmakers.

Adding to this roster, *Terrifier* (2016), directed by Damien Leone, broke into horror with the low-budget introduction of the sadistic Art the Clown. Its raw, disturbing scenes gained a cult following, leading to *Terrifier 2* (2022) and *Terrifier 3* (2024), making *Terrifier* a modern, low-budget horror franchise that shows you don't need big budgets to deliver big scares and healthy profits.

Filmmaker and comedian, Curry Barker, delivered an unexpected hit with *Milk & Serial*, a 62-minute horror feature about YouTube pranksters caught in a spiraling series of crises. Made on an $800 budget, the film showcases Barker and his comedy partner, Cooper Tomlinson, and is a prime example of how DIY horror can thrive with creativity and resourcefulness.

There are also people like my buddy Chris LaMartina. He was so in love with horror he held the boom for my *Two Front Teeth* movie when he was still in film school. I think he'd already made two movies as a high-schooler. While he may not be a household name like Sam Raimi, he's got lots of fans, and his *WNUF Halloween Special* (produced by my podcast co-host, Jimmy George) has become a Halloween staple for many of us. He and his supercool wife, Melissa, are still cranking out movies totally under his control and shipping them out of their house.

It's totally punk rock.

The reason all this works is because of horror fans. They're a rare breed. They're a little punk rock themselves. They collect Blu-Rays, they get horror tattoos, they celebrate when Spirit Halloween comes to town. They also slip on their black T-shirts and venture out to conventions to meet the stars of *Scare Jessica to Death* or *Basket Cases* or *The Night Watchmen*. And these kids are rabid. Most of them are chasing down every horror movie or book they can get their hands on. They thrive on finding that micro-budgeted gem and becoming its biggest fan before all the other freaks find it. They don't demand big-name stars or high-production values in their favorite movies either. Instead, they're on the hunt for unique original concepts, innovative storytelling, and effective scares. They're cool with something to check out on a Friday night... or something they'll rewatch every Halloween for the rest of their lives.

Because of them, trying your hand at some form of horror filmmaking is viable. I'm not really trying to sell you as much as celebrate the whole thing. If you're a DIY type, you know. Nothing I say could stop you anyway. If you're curious, you're probably one of us. And if you have zero interest, well, keep reading, you might bump into one of these unstoppable forces in your journeys. You might even option your book or screenplay to them!

SHORT FILMS

For some writers, writing a 100-page feature or a 70,000-word novel is daunting. Starting with something shorter is a no-brainer. While a full-blown discussion of crafting short stories and writing short films is outside of the scope of this book, it's fair to say many of the tactics from earlier chapters can be employed to full effect.

Most horror shorts contain the elements of the Monster in the House genre. Starting with a fresh monster, house, or sin can be a great way to brainstorm a unique concept. Put your vampire on an airplane or have a ghost haunt a bridge tollbooth or come up with a vengeful slasher who only kills people who park in handicapped spots... and you might have enough for a short.

You don't necessarily have to do a full-blown beat sheet. Sometimes you can just crank out a single scene once you get an idea. Using the Dread-O-Meter, scares, and gross-outs, you can break down a sequence that tells a short story.

Still, some shorts fail because they feel one-note. They don't have stake raisers or surprises. And while some shorts are so brief they can overcome these faults, I don't like to take any chances. I've worked on a bunch of anthology shorts and always use the *Save the Cat!* beat sheet.

Here's a quick beat sheet I did for the horror anthology *VHS*. This one—for the second movie, *VHS2*—is about a man with a GoPro on his head who gets turned into a zombie.

***VHS2*: A *Ride in the Park* Short Film *Save the Cat!* Beat Sheet**

Opening Image: From the view of a GoPro strapped to his helmet, we follow our hero on a wild mountain-bike ride jumping ramps.

Set-Up: The biker takes a break to talk to his girlfriend. This ride in the park is his ORDINARY LIFE. And from the GoPro footage, we realize this is going to be our POV for the mayhem that ensues.

Theme Stated: His girlfriend complains that he spends more time on the bike than he does with her. The story explores how we all get stuck in routines and obsessions that make us lose sight of what really matters, like relationships, personal growth, and happiness. The theme suggests that focusing on these meaningful aspects of life can help us break free from that "zombie fog" of distraction and live more fully.

Catalyst: A bloodied woman interrupts his day! As he helps her, she turns zombie and attacks. She bites him.

Debate: He fights her off and escapes into the woods. Dying, he stumbles. Falls. Gurgles. He goes still. And just when it seems like it all might be over for him...

Break into 2: Two bike riders appear. They ride over, thinking he needs help. As they attend to him, our hero jolts to life. He's a zombie now.

Fun & Games: He kills the bike-riding duo and has his first moments as a zombie. He tries to eat them, but as he's feasting, they wake up as zombies.

Now, as a new horde (of three), the trio shambles through the woods following a scent and cheerful voices.

Midpoint: The newly rotting zombies happen upon a child's birthday party at a park. The walking dead attack. It's a *false victory* because our guy is a zombie, but this cannibalistic way is pushing him further from his humanity.

Bad Guys Close In: The partiers scramble. The zombies chow down. Birthday attendees scavenge weapons. Our hero gets stabbed in the eye with a meat fork. And beaten with a Piñata bat. And gets his hand sizzled on the hot dog grill.

All Is Lost: At the window of a mini-van he's attacking, he catches a look at his reflection. He sees what he's become. He didn't quite realize the transformation until staring at his meat-fork- pierced eye in the reflection.

Dark Night of the Soul: As he ponders, he's blasted with a shotgun. It barely matters. He won't die. But now, he's stirred emotionally, *internal bad guys* playing on his dead soul. He hears crying... it reminds him of his girlfriend. He stumbles toward the girl and is pummeled by a speeding truck and run over.

Break into 3: His phone rings. His girlfriend is calling. Her voice gives him new hope.

Finale: He shoots himself.

Final Image: The lifeless camera captures the chaos of the changed world.

I cranked that out about an hour after the initial pitch was green-lit and pretty much it's what you see on screen in the anthology. I think the *Save the Cat!* beat sheet works great for shorts, so long as you don't get hung up on it for all the things you need in features. There's no need or time for B Stories, and character arcs, and *things that need fixing* can be slight. Typical multi-scene beats like the Finale can be single moments.

Another popular strategy is to take a larger feature or novel idea and just develop the Opening Image/Opening Scare as a self-contained mini-movie that serves as a proof of concept of your film. Imagine the classic opening of *Scream* or the terrifying start to *A Quiet Place* as a short film or a short story.

These projects can serve as proof-of-concepts or prototypes for larger endeavors or they can stand alone. Regardless, they allow for creators to refine their craft and build their portfolios and, perhaps with a little luck, they even serve as calling cards.

These types of shorts are usually anywhere from 3 to 10 minutes long—just enough to have some twists and turns and deliver a big final scare.

One example of a successful short film that transitioned into a feature-length project is *Lights Out*, written and directed by David F. Sandberg. The short, which revolves around a terrifying entity that only appears in the dark, gained attention online for its effective use of suspense and jump scares.

Lights Out is less than 3 minutes long. But even it can be tracked with a *Save the Cat!* beat sheet:

Lights Out Short Film _Save the Cat!_ Beat Sheet

Opening Image: A house at night. One light on. It's bedtime.

Set-Up: A woman is alone in her apartment, getting ready for bed.

Catalyst: In the hallway beside her bedroom, she flips a light off and sees a spooky thing standing in the shadows.

Debate: It jolts her. Was what she saw real? She flips the light on and off. Every time it's off, the creature is seen. And it moves a little closer and closer... until...

Break into 2: The creature is right up in her face!! Oh no, it's real.

Fun & Games: Okay, she should run far far away or get an exorcist. But this is a short and we don't have time for that. So, she makes a plan to get ready for bed, duct-taping the hallway light switch on and then hopping under the covers.

As she sleeps, something is running around the shadowy hall. Theater of the Mind. We hear the rip of the tape. The hall goes dark, leaving only the bedside light to protect her.

Midpoint: The woman covers her head with a blanket. As if that'll help. She's now in completely vulnerable territory. Trapped by a sea of darkness.

Bad Guys Close In: The woman peeks out, the thing creeping in on her.

All Is Lost: Buzzzzzzz... her bedside light flickers and goes out. The only thing keeping her safe.

Dark Night of the Soul: She hides under the blanket. It's not a great strategy, but it's her last defense. She whimpers and wallows. Surely, death is coming for her.

Break into Three: The light keeps buzzing and flickering. Curious, she sneaks a peek. The lamp's plug is loose in the power strip. If she can just plug it in all the way...

Finale: It's time to get brave. Battling her own courage, she moves from her safety blanket and reaches out into the danger zone to plug the lamp back in. She slowly reaches out and plugs it back in and stops the flickering.

She looks around. All is well. All seems back to normal. Maybe she will get some sleep.

Final Image: In an EVIL CONTINUES moment, she sees the hideous thing stalking her perched at the bedside lamp. It clicks off the light, leaving our hero alone in the dark and defenseless against the monster.

The balance between building dread and delivering scares or gross-outs greatly influences the effectiveness of your short. Whether you go the beat-sheet route for your story or not, if you're doing a one-scare sequence like *Lights Out*, I would recommend the Dread-O-Meter.

Dread-O-Meter for *Lights Out*

Dread, Scare or Gross-Out	Action/Description	Dread-O-Meter
Dread	A house at night. One light on. It's bedtime. (DARK & STORMY)	1
Dread	We see a woman alone in her apartment (ALL TOO QUIET), getting ready for bed wearing just her pajamas. (NAKED & NOT AFRAID)	3
Scare	In the hallway beside her bedroom, she flips a light off and sees a spooky thing standing in the shadows.	1
Dread	It jolts her. Was it real? She flips the light on and off. Every time it's off, the creature is seen. (SUMMONING THE BEAST) And it moves a little closer and closer... until...	4
Scare	Break into 2: The creature is right up in her face!! Oh no, it's real.	2

Dread, Scare or Gross-Out	Action/Description	Dread-O-Meter
Dread	Okay, she should run far, far away or get an exorcist. But this is a short and we don't have time for that. So, she makes a plan to get ready for bed, duct-taping the hallway light switch on and hopping under the covers, ready to sleep. (ENTERING THE KILLZONE)	3
Dread	But as she sleeps, something is running around the shadowy hall. (THEATER OF THE MIND) We hear the rip of the tape. The woman covers her head with a blanket. (EYES OFF THE PRIZE) As if that'll help. She's now in a completely vulnerable territory. Trapped by a sea of darkness.	4
Dread	The woman peeks out. (ALL TOO QUIET)	5
Dread	Buzzz... her bedside light flickers and starts to die out. This is bad. It's the only thing keeping her safe. (TECHNICAL DIFFICULTIES)	6
Dread	She hides under the blanket. It's not a great strategy, but it's her last defense. She whimpers and wallows. Surely, death is coming for her. (THEATER OF THE MIND)	7

Dread, Scare or Gross-Out	Action/Description	Dread-O-Meter
Dread	The light keeps buzzing and flickering. Curious, she sneaks a peek. The lamp's plug is loose in the power strip. If she can just plug it in. (FLICKERING LIGHTS)	8
Dread	It's time to get brave. Battling her own lack of courage, she moves from her safety blanket and reaches out into the danger zone (INTO THE KILL ZONE) to plug that thing back in.	9
Dread	She plugs it back in! She looks around. All is well. All seems back to normal. Maybe she will get some sleep. (ALL TOO QUIET)	10
Dread	She sees the hideous thing stalking her, perched at the bedside lamp. It clicks off the light, leaving our hero alone in the dark and defenseless against the monster.	Final Scare!

SHORT STORIES/SELF-PUBLISHING

Short stories work the same as short films. A couple years ago, Hollywood seemed hot on optioning short films like *Lights Out* to turn into feature films and TV. In recent years, Tinseltown has discovered a treasure trove of high-concept horror short stories online to scoop up for bigger projects. It's kind of cool. And easier than making a movie or writing a full screenplay or a novel. If you come up with a fresh new horror concept, it might be worthwhile to look into creating the short-story version first.

If you want to go the novelist path, there are several avenues. While traditional publishing can be a lucrative if not an uphill climb, the world of self-publishing can give a sense of satisfaction and complete control. My horror go-to guy, Adam Cesare, began his career by making things happen in the self-publishing and small-press world. He hustled his books at every MonsterCon and Creature Feature fest from here (Baltimore) to the Mississippi. He wrote a bunch of books and literally put them in fans' hands. This kind of passion and hard work led to a best-selling and Stoker Award-winning book, *Clown in a Cornfield*, which is now a full-fledged book series and has a feature film adaptation.

OTHER SPOOKY STUFF

Web series, narrative podcasts, graphic novels, and video games all operate under the same horror principles. Their producers or publishers are looking for well-crafted stories with great scares. I recommend considering them all. You never know where that big break is going to come.

BUT WHAT IF I REALLY WANT TO WORK WITH JAMES WAN AND MIKE FLANAGAN?

The path to working on studio horror and TV is long and has a lot of competition—no one can tell you what a sure-fire route to that lofty goal looks like.

Somebody once asked me what part of the filmmaking career got me most excited. I thought it would be when I sold my first script. It wasn't. Sure, the money helped! But the next day, I was still the same doubt-filled writer, guessing what my next move was.

Then I thought the most exciting thing would actually be getting on the set of something I wrote. And man, that was cool as hell, meeting people, seeing the circus; I'd highly advise if you get a movie green-lit, you ask to visit the set. You'll meet other filmmakers (networking!) and be inspired and learn a lot. But still, you'll be back to the grind the next day.

Well, maybe the most exciting thing would be when I saw the movie on the big screen and my name in the credits. For a lot of filmmakers, this can be the worst experience, spotting all the mistakes you made or all the jokes that didn't land and seeing people stare at their phones instead of watching your hard work.

I haven't risen to the heights of Leigh Whannell or Scott Derrickson or Jordan Peele, but I bet the accolades or the hits or the big deals aren't what fuels them... and even greats like Guillermo del Toro lament the dozens of projects that never got made. They experience a lot of the same frustration all of us do.

I know it's a cliché, but you can only control what you can control.

It took me a while to realize you have to love the process. Right now, I'm in my happy place, sitting on my coach typing words that you'll eventually read. I know it sounds weird, but this is my win.

Sure, I'm about to hit the save button and turn back to that treatment I'm working up for a creative exec, and then I have a meeting with a co-writer on a new spec. I'm still in the grind. And loving it.

The best advice I can give is not to worry about the results. Don't base your happiness on if you sell a script or get a novel published or get a job in a TV writers' room. Instead, focus on the person—the writer!—you want to be when you get that job. What are the skills you need to learn to become that person? What are the boundaries within yourself you need to push against? Maybe your writing is not up to the level. Maybe you're not good at pitching. Maybe you want to write personal scripts that transcend the genre. Maybe you lack confidence because there's a lot of filmmaking knowledge you don't have. Maybe it's more personal.

Think of where you want to be, figure out the type of writer who would be perfect for that position, and then go to work at it. Every day. Don't worry about the result. Worry about becoming that person.

There's one other step.

The big question you always get is "Why *you* for this project?"

I think asking yourself that is important. What is the reason you're driven to put in all this work and tons of time to develop yourself and make yourself the writer you've imagined?

It's usually a deep reason. For me, I think I always had the dream, but in the beginning, I never had the confidence or the support to go all in. At some point, that might have been the "why" for me. To prove to myself that I could pull it off if I focused and directed my passion, time, and energy into this career. I wanted to surprise myself and push it as far as it could go.

What's your deeper why?

Figure it out. And go make yourself that amazing writer who doesn't worry about results but is worthy and ready to handle 'em when they come.

BECAUSE THE EVIL NEVER DIES

First off, I have to thank the *Save the Cat!* folks, BJ Markel and Jason Kolinsky, for giving me a platform to follow in Blake Snyder's footsteps—and for all the hard work they put into editing, producing, and publishing these books. A huge thanks goes to Gina Mansfield for her brilliant design work, which made this book look every bit as sharp and professional as the rest of the *Save the Cat!* series.

I'd also like to thank my *Writers/Blockbusters* podcast buddies, Bob Rose and Jimmy George. This book was really born out of analyzing the dozens of horror scripts on our podcast. It was there I first came up with dread flags, and Jimmy conjured up one of the first Dread-O-Meters with *Jaws* (a version of which is seen in this book). I've learned so much from the guys and their focused analyses. There's probably enough material for 50 books in all the stuff we've done on the show—and it's all out there for free for you to listen to.

This book also had some great beta readers. Thanks to Chris LaMartina for giving me the idea to include "THE BIG SURPRISE." And to Tara Garwood for not only giving me some great feedback, but also being the first to put some of the book's tools to use in her own stories. Shoutout to Jenny Mollen as well, who read the book and immediately started applying its tools to her own screenplay in progress—an early vote of confidence that meant a lot.

And thanks to horror producer extraordinaire (among other genres) Craig Perry—the coolest guy in the biz but also a deeply knowledgeable and insightful horror fan—for giving me several suggestions and ideas that made this book that much better.